EVANGELICAL MISSIONS TOMORROW

EVANGELICAL MISSIONS TOMORROW

Edited by

Wade T. Coggins
E.L. Frizen, Jr.

William Carey Library

533 HERMOSA STREET • SOUTH PASADENA, CALIF. 91030

**Published by the William Carey Library
533 Hermosa Street
South Pasadena, Calif. 91030
Telephone 213-682-2047**

In accord with some of the most recent thinking in the academic press, the William Carey Library is pleased to present
this scholarly book which has been prepared from an author-
edited and author-prepared camera-ready manuscript.

Library of Congress Catalog Card Number 77-76525
International Standard Book Number 0-87808-156-9

PREFACE

This book contains a collection of articles by outstanding missions leaders in which they wrestle with a variety of issues confronting missionary work today and in the future.

The forum to which the writers addressed themselves when the articles were read as papers was a joint conference of three entities which have a common concern for the evangelization of the world and are involved in its implementation: the Interdenominational Foreign Mission Association, the Evangelical Foreign Missions Association and the Association of Evangelical Professors of Missions.

The conference was held September 27 – October 1, 1976 at Breech Training Academy, Overland Park, Kansas.

These papers were prepared to present to the conference and not for a book. The decision was made, however, to pull them together in a book making them available to a wider audience. Speed of publication has taken precedence over the desire for polished style.

The issues which are timely and crucial should prove valuable to all those who are vitally concerned about the outreach of the church. We offer them in the spirit of cooperation and sharing which characterized the conference itself.

WADE T. COGGINS, Executive Director – EFMA[*]
E.L. FRIZEN, JR., Executive Director – IFMA[*]

[*]See pages 195 through 197 for a description of the two organizations.

CONTENTS

1

THE GROUNDS FOR A NEW THRUST
IN WORLD MISSION

by Ralph D. Winter

As we prepare to confront the future, no matter what else we do we must 1) sum up our progress to the present, and 2) evaluate our program in the present. The first leads us to an awesome awareness of the task as yet unfinished, that is, the NEED. The second leads us to an impressive list of OBSTACLES to the meeting of that need. These two together--the massive NEED and the momentous OBSTACLES--constitute, in my opinion, the grounds for a major and imperative new thrust in missions, something we must immediately plan and pray for. Meanwhile, let us be asking ourselves whether what we are now doing is remotely close to what God can legitimately expect of evangelical forces in America today. Having just gone through all this material myself, I am deeply moved by the conviction that we must begin to talk in terms of actually doubling all that we are doing now. Nothing less will suffice. Let me try to show the basis on which I speak.

I will begin by pointing out the need--the unfulfilled dimensions of our task. This is the most important ground upon which to base a new thrust forward in world missions--I am a firm believer that the need as defined by the Great Commission is the call. But then secondly, I will hurry on to a series of twelve deadly obstacles that stand in our way in the reaching of that need. By acknowledging these obstacles, we will extend the grounds upon which we build our thesis--namely, that the agencies of mission--whether old or new--must now take the lead in a new forward thrust in world missions. First the NEED and then the OBSTACLES.

Ralph D. Winter, presently endeavoring to establish the "major mission center" to which this paper refers, was for ten years a field missionary in Guatemala and for another ten years on the faculty of the School of World Mission at Fuller Theological Seminary. He holds a Ph.D. from Cornell University and a B.S. in engineering from the California Institute of Technology. He is the editor of *Theological Education by Extension* and author of *The Twenty-Five Unbelievable Years*.

THE NEED

For me, the Great Commission is most significantly stated in three key texts: in Genesis 12:2,3; Isaiah 49:6, and Matthew 28:19,20. In all three cases the entire world, all the families of mankind--whether you call them nations, tribes, tongues, peoples, or whatever--are clearly in the picture. Two years ago at the International Congress on World Evangelization at Lausanne, I gave an address, the central thesis of which can be summed up in a single sentence: <u>while there are 2.7 billion people who do not even call themselves Christians, over 3/4 of them are beyond the range of any kind of normal (or "cultural -near-neighbor") evangelization by existing churches</u>. By "normal evangelism" I do not mean what is normally now being done; I refer as well to all of those various kinds of evangelism which believers in presently existing congregations <u>would be capable of launching</u> without surmounting unusual barriers of language and social structure. This "normal" evangelism has also been called "cultural-near-neighbor", as above, or mono-cultural evangelization, or E-0 and E-1 evangelism, and surely must continue and must even be vastly expanded. Let us distinguish, however, between E-0 evangelism (winning <u>nominal Christians</u> to Christ) and E-1 evangelism (winning people <u>who do not call themselves Christians</u> but who are in the same secular sphere as the church). Don't look now, but most evangelism is not even E-1, it is only E-0 evangelism among nominal Christians. The regional committees of the Lausanne Congress are hoping valiantly to expand at least E-0 and E-1 evangelism. But according to the analysis I presented two years ago, even assuming a great spiritual evangelizing revival were to sweep every existing congregation in the world, those congregations reaching out in normal evangelism could win all nominal Christians plus all people in their cultural sphere, but still be stopped short by culture barriers before reaching 3/4 of the non-Christians in the world today: <u>from that point on</u>, cross-cultural, E-2 and E-3 mission agencies would still be necessary.[1] This awesome fact was the main point I was attempting to communicate two years ago.[2]

But the particular relevance of this fact to a gathering of   mission executives is that in the providence of God <u>the mission society</u>, let me repeat, (whether denominational or interdenominational) is the only kind of organization which 2000 years of Christian experience assures us is able effectively to go <u>beyond</u> normal, E-0 or E-1, mono-cultural evangelism[3] and reach cross-culturally, by E-2 and E-3 methods, to the vast proportion of those who do not yet know Jesus Christ as Lord and Saviour.

The first diagram is a fairly exact scale drawing[4] representing the largest racial and cultural bloc of humanity--the Chinese. The large circle represents those Chinese who do not consider themselves Christians. The small circle outside the large circle represents the number of Chinese who do consider

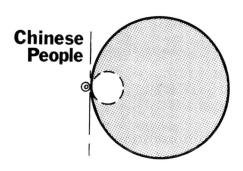

themselves Christians. The sphere within the small circle represents an estimate of the number of truly committed Chinese Christians--by this I do not mean, for example, all who call themselves evangelicals, but rather truly committed believers, specifically <u>those Christians on whom we may count to help finish the task</u>. (In passing, I might observe that a nominal evangelical is probably not much more likely to be of help in world evangelization than any other kind of nominal Christian, and all around the world it seems there are more nominal evangelicals every day.)

The first impression this diagram of the Chinese gives us is the vastness of the unfinished task. But a startling second message comes through to us when we note that the dotted circle within the large circle represents the limited number of Chinese whom even cross-cultural evangelists are able to get at during this present epoch of history. That is, the dotted circle represents the 40 million "overseas" Chinese, outside mainland China. But even if China were open, there is in Chinese society an amazing mosaic of sub-cultural barriers which would put most Chinese beyond the reach of normal evangelism as we have defined it.

Another large bloc of non-Christians is the Hindu. In this next diagram the large circle again represents non-Christians, this time the number of Hindus who do not consider themselves Christians. Note that here as in the case of the Chinese I am

referring to a culturally, not racially or religiously, defined
group. Thus we may say that the small circle outside the large
circle represents the number of people of Hindu cultural background who consider themselves Christians. Note carefully that

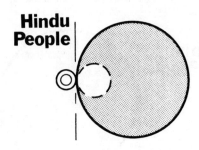

**Hindu
People**

this Christian circle is proportionately larger than in the case
of the Chinese. The sphere within the small circle (the committed Christians) is larger too, yet it is smaller relative to
the total number of Christians, that is, there are more nominal
Christians of Hindu background both absolutely and relatively.

Once more, if we are sensitive at all to the heart of God,
we must be stunned and crushed by the vastness of the unreached
populations within this major bloc of mankind. But the second
message is still more shocking: it is the stubborn fact not
often recognized that a relatively small number of people in
India are reachable by normal evangelistic efforts on the part
of even the Christians in India. These reachable people, represented by the dotted circle, are the Harijans--the remaining
non-Christians peoples in the formerly "untouchable" category.

Here especially let me emphasize once more that by normal
I do not mean what is now normally being done. A reliable--but
staggering--report indicates that 98% of all current evangelistic efforts in India, whether missionary or national, are not
even focused on non-Christians, but (as is true in the USA)
are attempts of believing Christians to reach nominal Christians
and bring them back into the vital fellowship of the church--
that is, Christians of the solid sphere reaching nominal Christians in the doughnut-shaped space around them. These are
specifically not efforts to reach even the people in the dotted
circle. But what a shame, because the dotted circle represents
the number of non-Christians of Hindu culture who are culturally
approachable by Christians, people with the same cultural tra-
ditions--shall we say caste? On the one hand, then, Christians
in India are not (with only rare exceptions) even attempting to

win totally non-Christian people. But on the other hand, if the Christians of India did suddenly and strenuously reach out to every last person within their various cultural traditions, they would not even in that hypothetical case be able to win anyone outside of the circle with the dotted line unless, note, unless they made new beachheads by the utilization of what would substantially be traditional missionary techniques (involving the establishment of the kind of professional agencies capable of crossing seriously high cultural barriers).

At the risk of elaborating this point unnecessarily, let me be very sure what I am saying is clear. All countries have their caste systems. Sometimes the barriers are linguistic differences, economic differences or other types of cultural differences. The barriers of this type are almost always socially describable. They are not spiritual barriers. While the spiritual barriers are the same whether a nominal Christian becomes committed to Christ or a total non-Christian becomes committed to Christ, the cultural barriers, where they exist, are always a stubborn technical problem in addition. In India, as in many other countries, the vast bulk of Christians are found in a relatively small number of social groupings, and it is always a problem for them to cross the culture barriers into other groups. For example, the most integrated of all Indian churches may well be the Church of South India, which embraces 100 different castes. Yet to this day 95 percent of its members derive from only five castes, all of which represent the Harijan or formerly "untouchable" category. This, then, is why we must urgently face the fact that special types of E-2 and E-3 cross-cultural evangelistic efforts (well known in this gathering) will be necessary if any significant proportion of the middle and higher castes are ever to be reached. This is why the dotted circle is dismayingly small in the case of India. Thus something different, decisively different, urgently more, must be done to reach the vast bulk of the Indians for Christ.

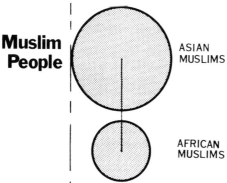

Muslim People

ASIAN MUSLIMS

AFRICAN MUSLIMS

The third large non-Christian cultural tradition of mankind is pictured in this next diagram. Since there are huge
numbers of Muslims both in Africa and Asia, we have used two
circles to depict the non-Christians of Muslim cultural background. In this case a curious and tragic fact appears: there
are not enough Christians of Muslim extraction that we can even
depict them in a small circle as we did for the Chinese and the
Hindus. For one thing, a highly disturbing fact is that up to
now in mission history we have either not <u>known</u> how or have not
been <u>able</u> to achieve the development of a "Muslims for Jesus"
movement, anywhere, with one or two possible exceptions. On
the one hand, we have all become accustomed to hearing about
Jews for Jesus, and there are from 10 to 30 thousand such people
in the United States--this despite the fact that they were
brought up from infancy to react against the name of Jesus Christ.
The amazing difference on the other hand is that Muslims are
brought up to revere Jesus highly. Their holy book, the Koran,
technical scholars today point out actually elevates Jesus above
Mohammed. But to date there are very few Muslims for Jesus.
How tempted I am to throw away the rest of my notes and just tell
about some of the possibilities in this area. But that will have
to wait.

We have now seen three major blocs of non-Christians, and
in each case only a tiny proportion of the people in these blocs
represent people whose social groupings would allow them easily
to become part of (and also attract their friends to) any existing congregation of believers in Christ on the face of the earth.
To sum up, normal evangelism, even if effectively and fully
launched from all present congregations,is totally inadequate to
grapple with this major part of the unfinished task. A group
of mission executives must surely be the group which God expects
to take this fact most seriously.

Now, once we have recognized the existence of these three
major groups, the remaining, or "other" non-Christians in Asia
represent (by contrast) only a mopping-up operation.

Other Asian Peoples

The astonishing novelty in this diagram is the large
number of Christians culturally related to the remaining non-
Christians. The number of Christians is of a totally different
magnitude and proportion than in the previous diagrams. As
before the sphere within the circle of Christians represents an
estimate of the number of committed believers. This group also
is vastly larger. Who are the peoples in this catch-all group
of "other" non-Christian Asians? There are, for example, 100
million Japanese. Are they all reachable by "normal" evangelism? Lest we exaggerate the number requiring cross-cultural
evangelism, let us recall that while there are some fairly
momentous cultural barriers to be crossed in the winning of all
Japanese into the present variety of existing Japanese churches,
such cultural barriers are in no way comparable to the barriers
that prevent normal evangelism from even touching the vast bulk
of the Hindus or the Muslims. Thus the dotted circle--people
who can (even conceivably) be reached by normal evangelism--is
very much larger and includes not only many Japanese but also
many Buddhists for whom there are in fact viable Christian traditions nearby that do not present a major social obstacle to
their affiliation. In this estimate we are certainly not over
but under estimating the proportions of those who cannot be
reached by normal (E-0 or E-1) evangelism.

Let us now move on to the last bloc of non-Christians outside of the Western world. We have already mentioned the non-
Christian Muslims of Africa. This diagram shows the non-Christians of Africa who are not Muslims. Recalling that Africa was
only 3% Christian in 1900, we stand amazed and pleased that the

Other African Peoples

number of Christians is getting close to being equal to the
number of non-Christians who are not Muslims! The number of
committed Christians is large too.

In view of these general contours for Asia and Africa, let
us put them in a single chart and note the amazingly different
proportions in the Western world. Page 8 breaks the Western
world down by isolating the population of the USA into a separate diagram. Since these circles are drawn on the same scale as

WESTERN WORLD
(EUROPE, RUSSIA, AMERICAS, AUSTRALIA , NEW ZEALAND)

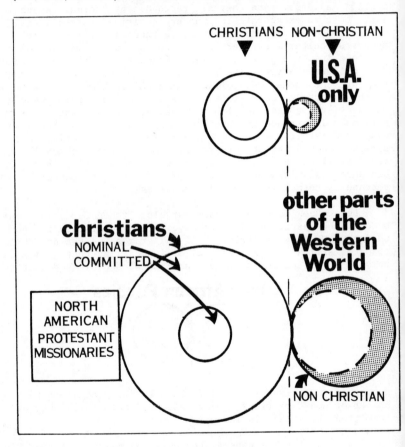

Numerical data from which these drawings are made
is found on page 25.

NON·WESTERN WORLD
(= ASIA , AFRICA)

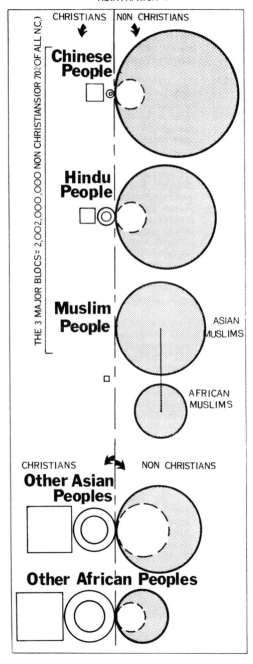

THE 3 MAJOR BLOCS = 2,002,000,000 NON CHRISTIANS(OR 70% OF ALL N.C.)

CHRISTIANS   NON CHRISTIANS

Chinese People

Hindu People

Muslim People

ASIAN MUSLIMS

AFRICAN MUSLIMS

CHRISTIANS   NON CHRISTIANS

Other Asian Peoples

Other African Peoples

before, we see immediately that the Western world contains most
of the nominal Christians. We can verify by eye the fact that
85% of the nominal Christians are in the West while only a little
over half of the committed Christians are in the West. It is
even more obvious that the ratio of Christians to non-Christians
is radically different in the Western world when compared to
every area of Asia and Africa except non-Muslim Africa. Here
then are the hard facts that maintain the credence of that long
useful adage that where there are 10 men at one end of a log and
only one at the other, the priorities are obvious, especially
if the ten men are at the smaller end of the log. Fully to
digest these diagrams can rightly absorb hours and hours of deep
thought and earnest prayer. Here in scale drawing is the primary
need, in terms of missionary strategy, in the world today. However, before moving on, let us stop to recognize the following:
1) the great bulk of people on this planet are concentrated
in Africa and Asia; 2) an even greater proportion of Africa and
Asia (than the Western world) consists of peoples who do not
consider themselves Christian; 3) the three largest cultural
blocs of mankind--the Chinese, Hindus and Muslims--have only
tiny Christian communities, if any at all, related to them;
4) in the case of China and India, only a very small proportion
of the non-Christians are within normal evangelistic striking
range of the existing Christians: and 5) despite the small number of Christians from within these large cultural traditions,
their evangelistic efforts to evangelize are mainly soaked up by
the spiritual needs of the nominal belt that surrounds them.
Once we size up the need in these terms, it must be clear that
the only effective answer to the major part of this need can come
from specialized cross-cultural organizations of the type represented by a standard mission society, either local or foreign.
The vast millions of people in the doughnut-shaped areas of the
Western world, for example, absorb almost the entire energies of
evangelism on the part of the committed Christians in those areas.
It is safe to say that a high percentage of all the people being
converted to Christ in the Western world have all along considered
themselves Christian. Since dealing with nominal Christians is
the kind of evangelism most American Christians are acquainted
with, it is not surprising that Americans who become involved in
traditional foreign missions generally have a tough time figuring
out how to do cross-cultural evangelism, and even if they do
figure it out, have an even tougher time explaining to people
back home how different pioneer missionary work is from the
normal evangelism of cultural near-neighbors.

In these words I have no desire whatsoever to belittle the
immensity of the commonly understood task of bringing about
spiritual renewal among lifeless nominal Christians. This task
of renewal is not only big, it is truly urgent, because world-

wide outreach to non-Christians is considerably blunted by the
scandalous behaviour of nominal Christians back home in the
Western world. Such reasoning helps understand the similar
nominal gap in the Christian churches in Africa and Asia. Nominal Christians emerge automatically in the second generation
and seem everywhere eventually to ring the Christian church
around like a soft doughnut, which then in turn prevents the
committed Christians from even getting out beyond that doughnut
to the non-Christian world. This is again the reason why we
have suggested that unless something specific is done on the
order of special organizations of the type represented by the
mission societies, no truly effective outreach to totally non-
Christian people is likely to be significantly strong. Christian groups, even those which are relatively highly committed,
often tend to be so cozy that it takes special organizations
for renewal even to shake them up and get them to witness to
the nearby nominal Christians.

Thus the blunt truth is that if you had to guess at the
proportion of all the evangelizing energies of evangelicals
around the world expended on the renewing of nominal Christians
you would probably come up with something like 97%. Yet,
nominal Christians, though numerous, are only about one-fourth
as numerous as the total of nominal Christians and non-Christians.
Why should the nominal one-fourth receive 97% of all evangelizing energies? Furthermore, it is incomparably more difficult
to work cross-culturally: the larger job is not only larger
but harder--unimaginably more difficult in regard to the pre-
requisites of special training and preparation required for any
real success.

As a final element in this presentation of the need, let
us consider the number of full-time missionaries who are working
in the various areas of the world. I have useable data [5] only
for North American missionaries. (See rectangles on pp. 8 and 9.)
If we were to use the same scale I have already used, the number
of missionaries could not even be seen. Thus, while the family
of circles on all these charts represents masses of people, the
squares, on a completely different scale,[6] represent proportionate numbers of North American missionaries. This adds a whole
new dimension requiring earnest and urgent prayer and reflection.
Notice the relatively small number of missionaries at work with
the Chinese and the Hindus, the almost microscopic number who
are working with Muslims, and the relatively huge numbers of
missionaries working with "other Asians" and in non-Muslim
Africa--exactly where most of the national Christians already
are. As a result, it is not difficult to understand how it
may be claimed that the average missionary today is no more
likely to be fulfilling a ministry directly among non-Christians

than are his supporters back home. You will quibble about this
statement. You will say, "But they are at least back-stopping
nationals who are on the evangelistic cutting edge." (But we
have already noted that the nationals are working mainly with
nominal Christians.) You will say it is not true of your
mission. But I humbly ask you to wrestle with these claims--
that most missionaries are first of all located where there
are by now many, many Christians, and secondly, that most of
them are working most of their time with the Christians rather
than devoting their primary attention to scaling the barriers
defending the non-Christian world. This is by no means the
fault merely of the mission agencies, much less of the missionaries, since national Christians often try desperately to keep
missionary aid to themselves. But it is undeniable that some
of the most pervasive trends in the past 50 years have been
1) the successful and impressive development of the national
churches, 2) the waning percentage of pioneer-type missionary
recruits, and 3) the increasing demands by the national churches
for missionary specialists to work in the area of nurture. As
a result, the front line evangelical missionary today may not
be as extinct as the dodo, but is far less visible than the
general practitioner in medicine. It is eminently fair to say
that most present-day missionaries are specialists working in
tasks other than cross-cultural evangelism among totally non-
Christian people. We do well not to assume that this ought to
be the case. This may be the welcome "new day" in relation to
national churches, but it represents a massive, mainly tragic
swerving away from the straightforward requirements of the unfulfilled task in regard to the 2.8 billion non-Christians.

These diagrams thus depict the stark reality of the unfinished task. The root problem is not as likely to be too
many missionaries in any one place as it is to be too few in
others. I am not here questioning the validity or strategic
value of what most missionaries are doing. My purpose in this
first heading is simply to point out that in relation to the
major bastions of the need, we are only touching the hem of
the garment.

Finally, what these diagrams do not show is the vast number
of organizations that are focusing on nominal Christians in the
United States. The squares we have drawn only show the number
of North American missionaries working outside of North America.
There are perhaps 300 or 400,000 full-time Christian workers
within the United States, and of the estimated 60 million
committed Christians, perhaps 2 million highly evangelistic
individual Christians, but out of all of this evangelizing
energy virtually none is focused upon people who are totally
non-Christian. Indeed, if I were to guess, I would have to say

that even the number of EFMA/IFMA missionaries overseas who are
effectively dealing with totally non-Christian populations would
be less than one out of 15, or about 1,000, while the number of
full-time Christian workers in the U.S. deriving from the same
evangelical constituency but who are focusing on Christian
nurture or evangelism of nominal Christians at home would number
30,000, perhaps twice that. That is, at least 80 times as many
people. But what does all this mean? It means that even though,
as we have seen, the unfinished task of reaching the totally non-
Christian people of the world is both immensely _larger_ and immensely _harder_, we in the U.S. are devoting to it only 1/80th of our
specifically Evangelical full-time task force.

All of this then sums up the nature and the scope of the
need. But notice, if the need is the call, then it is our
bounden duty to ask an additional question: why in this hour of
great challenge and opportunity are we American Christians not
heeding the call? Why are we doing less in proportion to our
available potential than at any time in the last hundred years?
It is time to bestir ourselves anew. It is time for a whole new,
doubling thrust forward.

If we respond to the call, we will then eagerly and zeal-
ously scrutinize the _obstacles_ between us and the meeting of this
need.

THE OBSTACLES

There are many obstacles; there always have been. I have
selected a deadly dozen which confront Evangelical missions
today and which Evangelical mission agencies must do something
about if there is going to be a major new successful thrust in
world missions. I have called these _obstacles_ or _problems_, but
some of them are simply closed doors that we must merely reach
out and open. Not all of these problems can be solved directly
by the agencies or by the agencies alone, but in all cases, I
believe, the mission agency and what it does is the most strategic source of the larger solution.

1. _The Bare-Handed Missionary_. This problem can involve
the mission agency, the home church, and the missionary on the
field. How does it happen? In many circles the number of
missionaries sent out controls the amount of money that can be
raised. Personalized giving is not only a healthy, but a relatively easy way to raise money. But when some churches refuse
to give money to anything but people, and never to projects,
and when field budgets are chronically limited and missionaries
have barely enough for their own support, this easy road will
actually be the hardest of all in terms of field accomplishments.
Some people may even feel that their mission giving is simply

for the purpose of paying unfortunate missionaries to flail
against impossible odds, and the resulting vicarious sense of
suffering becomes merely a bizarre therapy to the guilt-ridden,
affluent society that provides the funds. But if every mission-
minded church supported just <u>people</u>, it would wreck the cause
of missions. Thus, a significant obstacle to the fulfillment
of the Great Commission is the continuing unwillingness of many
churches to acknowledge that while they may well be <u>missionary</u>
minded, they are not yet <u>mission</u> minded. They care about the
missionary, for various reasons, but they do not yet properly
care about his work or his true success. I feel the mission
agencies must take the lead, working both directly with the
churches and also indirectly through the Association of Church
Missions Committees[7], to do everything in their power to re-
educate the churches in regard to work budgets and other projects.

     2. <u>The Self-Managing Missionary</u>. A second obstacle to a
great new thrust is the desperate inefficiency of the daily work
of the average missionary. After many years of thinking about
this and interviewing missionaries in different parts of the
world, I believe this sort of inefficiency is far more likely to
be a major obstacle to real accomplishment than any spiritual
factor. The lack of vital supervision overseas continues partly
because of the desire of every mission agency to avoid unnecessary administrative staff and to put as many missionaries on the
front line as possible, which in part is bowing to the romantic
expectations of the churches. Thus, some missions unconsciously
compete with one another in seeing how low a percentage their
administrative overhead can be. However, it is a simple fact
of human nature that practically no one can do his best if he
is completely his own boss. This is the chief reason, we are
told, why three out of four small businesses fail in the U.S.:
people, most people, cannot effectively self-manage. Pity the
poor missionary reading a book on self-management! I believe
that one-half of all missionaries are seriously failing to live
the ordered, disciplined and efficient lives that they themselves would like to live. The average missionary's desk is a
shambles. As a result he lives in a constant spiritual battle
between what he is and what he knows he could be. Spiritual
problems are, as I have already suggested, more often effects
than causes. No commercial firm would let a man work with so
little supervision and it is not a matter of trust, but support.

     There are many reasons for this phenomenon. One is the
extreme individualism of the American culture. Another is the
extended period of student experience (running through a quarter
of a century for many) during which a student never works under
or over anyone. Perhaps as a result a great emphasis has

gradually developed on individual guidance. Eventually such students often go out as missionaries with the idea that God only guides people and not organizations, and yet in truth it may be more often the other way around. We might even define the "prayer closet junky" as the student who doesn't avail himself of any other person's influence or judgment and ends up on the field totally unprepared to obey an organization. The kind of supervision I am saying is needed doesn't have to be paternalistic, nor complicated, nor expensive. Many a missionary would be able to straighten out his life if there were only someone to whom he could report monthly--someone who would not tell him what to do but would simply and firmly help him keep track of his own acknowledged priorities and objectives. What a tragedy that so relatively simple a problem to remedy could continue to be such a major obstacle to spiritual health as well as a major block to significant accomplishment in missions today.

3. The Untrained Missionary. While we're talking about missionaries, a third obstacle is the missionary who feels and knows he is untrained. I am not thinking so much now about inadequate pre-field training as I am about the general absence of long-term in-service training. Missionary Internship and the Toronto Institute of Linguistics are excellent examples of pre-or mid-service agencies. But missionaries are virtually abandoned the rest of the time. I am involved in a program called the Church Growth Book Club that each year sends out to missionaries around the world a quarter of a million dollars worth of books on mission strategy. However, I know that, circumstances being what they are, these books are rarely read. Thus these purchases represent the pathetic reaching out of missionaries who have rising expectations about their own need for special education. But for most of them their own mission has no policy that approves or supports their effective use of this vast new flood of superb materials, and in some cases it may in fact be the overworked, harassed executive back home who is furthest behind in this area. Some U.S. schools are offering the opportunity for credit-bearing courses to be done in-service. Personnel secretaries are aware that recent recruits have a whole new set of career and educational expectations that are unprecedented. Unless agencies rise to meet these new expectations, we may allow serious damage to take place.

4. The Rise of the Questioning Layman. The very appearance of an unprecedented but surely welcome flood of specialized literature on missions relates to another problem area which urgently requires attention if there is to be a correspondingly unprecedented new thrust in missions. It is the rise of the questioning layman. Some of these people actually get and read the books I've just mentioned before the missionaries do. They

may not entirely understand them but they begin asking questions
which are not easily or quickly answered. [7] In this regard the
Association of Church Missions Committees [7] has suddenly risen
out of nowhere and is now an unstoppable major force. Many
church mission committees are now sending out questionnaires to
missionaries and mission boards that take days to fill out. If
every church did this, the entire mission movement around the
world would stop dead in its tracks. Wesley Duewel of OMS
International has written what I consider to be the classical
answer to the wrong kind of investigation on the part of the
local church. But his letter by itself is merely the answer,
not the solution to the problem. Local church people are at
this moment tramping around the world as tourists, poking their
noses in everywhere not often fully understanding what they see,
and we live in the age of Ralph Nader! This looming obstacle
to harmony and teamwork between churches and missions is not
going to blow away like a fad. Agencies must face this squarely.
They must ultimately welcome the new depth of knowledge in many
lay circles. They must recognize and support the ACMC as a
means of strengthening lay people's grasp of the real problems,
and deepening their confidence in the professional agencies
whose work is so essential to the task.

     5. <u>Failure to Harness Vital New Forces</u>. This leads to a
fifth obstacle, for which there are divergent examples. It is
in part the failure to hand leadership down to a younger generation. Many of us in this room were already adults in the
Second World War. Many missions today are top heavy with older
missionaries, if you would diagram their age structure in one
large denominational board, 90% are over 45 years old. Yet
God in the past two decades has been raising up thousands of
young people who could and should have become dynamic missionaries today and tomorrow, most of whom have been shunted off
elsewhere or perhaps reluctantly dealt with in low priority,
ineffective short term programs. One result is a whole new
type of mission like Operation Mobilization and Youth with a
Mission, and you name it. People sent out each year by such
agencies already virtually outnumber the tally of all traditional missionaries under EFMA or IFMA, especially if you sub-
tract the short termers now within the EFMA/IFMA spheres.

     Why has this happened? For one thing, many a traditional
agency is having a tough time in its transition from older to
younger leadership. This task of successful leadership succes-
sion is somewhat parallel to the delicate task of turning things
over to the nationals on the field. But in regard to absorbing
the young people of today, I sincerely believe that the ordinary church-planting mission agency would not be wise to move

forward into the future without at least developing a junior division which could work alongside of the present framework without being totally submerged. But this is a big subject.

Any list of vital forces to be harnessed should also include the inability of Third World young people to find experienced Third World mission structures to supervise them, not just support them on the field. Only a few days ago an Asian mission leader who has tried to solve this problem told me that he had visited around at several veteran mission headquarters in the States, asking in vain if a Korean division could be added to their ranks, supported by Korean churches, but supervised and coordinated in the field by the older and experienced Western agency. This sort of thing would, of course, be a transitional arrangment. But I am desperately convinced that great resources of Third World youth, as well as American youth, will be lost if the veteran agencies cannot allow them to collaborate in new ways in subordinate, semi-autonomous divisions. Charlie Mellis's new book, Committed Communities, Fresh Springs for World Outreach sheds a lot of light in this area. (William Carey Library, South Pasadena, CA 1977)

Failure to harness new forces is reflected in part in the breaking forth of a new category of non-professional mission agencies--that is to say, agencies that do not employ veteran missionaries in their leadership or field force. In this category fall such activities as World Vision, which started out in areas supplementary to traditional work. Or the John Haggai Institute in Singapore, which seeks to supplement traditional mission work. Or take new recent approaches like the new worldwide network of Lausanne Committees on Evangelism. Or what about the Agape Program of Campus Crusade, or the World Literature Crusade, or Christian Aid Mission in Washington? All such agencies to one extent or another bypass intentionally or unintentionally the traditional missionary apparatus--sometimes with good reason. But the nearly total absence of their leadership in IFMA/EFMA circles does not auger well for a massive new thrust in missions. There must somehow be a period of romance, courtship and marriage between these two streams.

6. The Need for Dual-Board Non-Western Missions. We stand at the threshold of a new era which either will or will not harness the vast resources of the mission lands themselves in cross-cultural mission outreach. If we fail to make sure this will happen, that failure may constitute a truly unsurmountable obstacle to the great new thrust that must be launched. The general subject of Third World Missions is well known, and there are two new books on the subject--one written and the other edited by Marlin Nelson.[8] To the current perceptions you

all have, let me add just one observation: I have myself long
thought of Western missions and non-Western missions as being
essentially parts of two separate worlds. But I have recently
noticed that from almost every mission land you can name there
are now many thousands of people in the United States, more of
them more often in Southern California than in any other place.

There are for example more Filipino medical doctors in the
U.S. than in the Philippines. It seems perfectly logical that
the Evangelicals among the thousands of Filipinos in the U. S.
should not only volunteer for and support missions to and from
their own people, but should form in this country one side of
a dual-board relationship. For a long time there has been a
mission board operated by Japanese in Los Angeles coordinated
with efforts to and from Japan. There is more recently the
China Graduate School of Theology with both a U.S. and a Hong
Kong board, both predominantly Chinese.

Perhaps this is a new and fertile pattern which, with the
friendly cooperation of the veteran agencies, can be advanced
and enhanced far more than at present. We seem to hear constantly about the non-Christian foreign students in our midst,
and we are increasingly aware of thousands of wonderful Christians in the mission lands. What about the wonderful foreign
Christians who are no longer over there but right here? Somehow American evangelicals haven't adjusted in a friendly way to
the fact that the percentage of Christians among the foreigners
who are eagerly invading America for permanent residence is
far higher than the percentage of Christians in the lands they
come from. Instead of frowning on them for leaving their
countries, let us work and pray for their active involvement at
least in supporting Third World missions of their own kind
through an American dual board, or perhaps joining in the task
themselves as full-fledged missionaries with a new self-respect
we now tend to deny them.

We already all know that mission agencies must be sure
churches are planted on the field. We are now realizing that
missions must also be planted on the field. But is your agency
prepared to help a new American board into existence to coordinate itself with a Third World mission? Be careful you do not
think I am referring here to what is also happening--Third
World agencies establishing U.S. offices to raise money from
Anglo-Americans.

7. The Decline of Women's Involvement. Another obstacle
to the highest achievement of a major thrust in missions is
surely the continued decline of women's involvement. Don't
look now, but women in mission leadership are virtually gone

from the picture compared to their active presence a half century ago. I don't mean to ignore all the valiant missionary
wives, but I am talking about a much more prominent level of
initiative. Except for Beaver's book, <u>All Loves Excelling</u>,[9]
the rise of American women in missions beginning in 1850 and
ending in 1950 is virtually an untold story. Absolutely nothing
in the world of missions today is likely to produce another
8,000 student women's university such as the one in Seoul, Korea.
Why should women's initiative, women's vitality, women's leadership so spectacular a half century ago be virtually absent
from missions today? Even pastors' and missionaries' wives are
less involved in the work. In 1910 there were 40 evangelical
boards of missions operated totally by single women. Today
there is not one. Perhaps only the mission historians recall
that single women were once actively successful in many situations where married people simply cannot do the job. But the
phenomenon is not a case of single <u>women</u> alone. Protestant
missions in recent years have made <u>little</u> or no effective use
of single people in general, especially single men, even
though we might have noticed that single people have a higher
percentage of disposable income! Is it not curious that
Roman Catholics think they can do almost entirely without
married people while Protestants think they can do almost entirely without single people? In three out of four open doors
in missions today unentangled single people could more readily
than married people be the first and best to penetrate. I don't
mean going out alone. But I'm sorry there is not time here to
explore just how we might surmount this obstacle.

8. "<u>Every Organization for Itself</u>". Another major obstacle is the syndrome of every-organization-for-itself. We all
have the right theology of the church; we believe in the body
of Christ and that one member cannot say to the other, "I have
no need of thee"; but we sometimes act as if each agency is a
self-sufficient body of its own. True, mission agencies need
autonomy and mobility; they need to mind their own business, or
no one else will. But they do in fact live and move in a larger
whirl of other missions, other churches, and other organizations
of all kinds, all of which <u>together</u> constitute the body of
Christ--the church. I have spent great effort in trying to
clarify in my writings that the word <u>church</u> rightly understood
includes all Christian organizations, not just those that
(often with a tinge of presumption) call themselves churches.
But what is the use of agencies finally achieving theological
legitimacy as a regular part of the church if they then accept
no responsibility beyond their own activity?

We have referred already to those churches which pursue
the highest of mission budgets, but raise money only for

individuals. Well, what about mission agencies that have no
history of lending anybody to any other cause? The CBFMS has
lent more people than any other mission I know of, lent them to
causes that vitally affect many missions but that otherwise fall
between the cracks. And we must salute those service agencies
like Overseas Crusades that have an excellent record of working
in cross-pollenization as servants among missions and churches.
Or how about the Christian and Missionary Alliance church-planting youth movement in the Philippines that plants churches for
several different denominations? And, since I'm not in the pay
of IFMA or EFMA, let me say frankly that I can see no particular value whatsoever in the member agencies of IFMA and EFMA
keeping these associations so poor. What thrilling possibilities there are in the many existing joint committees (and
others that need to be established) if they just had a little
more muscle. We are all limping in ways we could be leaping
if only we could cooperate more effectively in a number of
ways. Would your agency lend a full-time missionary to a
joint IFMA-EFMA committee? I had a vision or a dream a few
days ago, as I was mulling over this subject. I imagined a
soldier moving past a wounded buddy, saying, "Sorry, I can't
stop to help you--I'm trying for a silver medal." Surely
what Jesus said to individuals applies to agencies: "if an
agency seeks to save its own life, it shall lose it, but if
any agency shall lend its people or give its funds to causes
beyond its immediate needs, it shall grow and abound." Can we
believe and act on this?

9. <u>The Lack of a Major Mission Center</u>. This leads me to
a project very close to my own heart. I am not sure that there
is anything I am presently doing that would be so great a contribution to the Great Commission if I could only get support
to work full time in this new project. I speak of the need for
the establishment of a major mission center, the primary purpose of which would be to focus new, major attention on the
Chinese, Muslim and Hindu groups. If every mission agency represented here were to lend one key person, such a center could
jump into being. The idea to which I refer has been talked
about now for two years, and an open discussion tomorrow noon
will take it further. It involves the availability of a major
former college campus in Pasadena, and would be in no way
bound to any denomination, school, or mission structure. I
would hope that it might beautifully complement, in the area
of <u>the work of the world's mission agencies</u>, the emphases of
the Billy Graham center on the <u>evangelistic outreach of the
world's churches</u>. I hope when you get a chance to read the
tentative description of this center[10], you will think seriously

and urgently about your agency lending a key person and thus be
in on the ground floor. One of the novel aspects of the center
will be its avowed attempt to bring about a wedding between the
professional missionary tradition and the university tradition
within which more and more missionaries are being processed and
formed. But with that hint let me rush on to the tenth obstacle.

   10. <u>The Absence of Economically Indigenized Projects</u>.
Both foreign governments and national churches are getting more
and more demanding in regard to just who it is that comes to
work among them. Secular missionaries emanating from American
universities nowadays far outnumber the spiritual missionaries
in most places around the world. It is said that all Americans
other than missionaries outnumber missionaries 105 to 1 in the
non-Western world. Some governments want to be very sure that
a foreign worker brings something that will not displace
national workers. Such governments may in some ways appreciate,
but at the same time suspect, the people whose work is supported
from a foreign country with who-knows-what purposes lurking
behind it. For example, a missionary radio station receiving
all its support from home can go on broadcasting forever without
listening to its listeners. But the same is true for any other
kind of service. There is something intrinsically cumbersome
about a service that is paid for by someone other than those
being served. A delightful book that rocks the perspectives of
the average American mission leader is called <u>Profit For The</u>
<u>Lord</u>.[11] It describes the work of two European missions that have
planted not only churches but economic enterprises designed
from the start to be turned over. Thus they do not take jobs
away from nationals but create jobs for them. The American
missionary tradition has been curiously reluctant to found
anything but projects like schools, hospitals, and radio stations, which are, in fact, the most difficult of all to turn
over as self-supporting enterprises. A missionary nurse (in a
field where I <u>did not</u> work) once told me that "you cannot mix
love and business." But where did she study missions? It has
been done and it must be done. The Apostle Paul did it;
William Carey did it; all the early Moravian missionaries did
it--they founded whole cities like Bethlehem, Pennsylvania.
Where have we been? If we cannot get in and master this dimension it will remain a major obstacle to the development of
sufficient muscle in the massive thrust that is necessary. The
hundreds of thousands of Americans that outnumber us overseas
today are virtually all supported directly by the work they do.
Note well that I am not really talking about non-professional
missionaries tying in with secular companies. I am referring
to what Interlink in Wheaton is trying to do--mainly unnoticed
and unaided or at least unparalleled by the veteran agencies.
This goes far beyond tent-making. In a word: we need to help

into being thousands of companies owned and operated by national
believers. If nothing else, Third World missions will depend
on, and wait for this kind of development for their life blood
in the future. This explains why affluent Korean and Hong Kong
Christians are now able to send their own missionaries.

11. The Myth of Over-Missionizing. An eleventh obstacle
is mainly psychological. It is the totally unsupported sensation
that in general missionaries are somehow not wanted or are too
numerous in the non-Western countries. In order to prove this
myth, small incidents are sometimes blown all out of proportion.
We must fight back with hard facts. Explain to me how a small
Arab country bitterly revulsed by the drinking habits and
sexual license rampant in the Western world would nevertheless
willingly invite in and pay for the presence of so many Western
technicians that its own citizens are literally outnumbered in
their own country. The country I refer to is the United Arab
Emirates, with only 225,000 citizens but which has now 235,000
Westerners working there as invited guests, paid for by oil
income. If a country like that can stand for over 200,000
outsiders, would 100 specially trained missionaries be too many,
missionaries who would understand and respect Muslim traditions
and at least not drink and carouse?   Be careful if you say yes,
because by using the same ratio of missionaries to citizens
(e.g., 100 per 200,000) we must conclude that there is room for
100,000 missionaries in North Africa and the Middle East. Again,
there is not space to discuss the challenging implications of
this potentiality. Thus, while there may be too many Westerners
in some countries, the missionary is in fact comparatively rare,
even though he is of all foreigners least likely to be resented
across the board. Furthermore as we saw earlier, for most
non-Christians of the world there is neither evangelistic nor
missionary outreach.

12. The Massive Omission. The twelfth obstacle I shall
refer to confronts us once again with the vast need with which
we began. It is the simple fact that the existing apparatus
of missions, whether Western or Third World, is mainly occupied
with the nurture of Christians, with the winning to Christ of
nominal Christians, or at best with outreach into nearby areas
and culturally similar peoples which represent only a small
percentage of the remaining need. Either major new mission
agencies, many of them, must be founded, or major new emphases
(or divisions) of existing agencies must soon be established if
we are even going to begin to treat fairly the Chinese, Hindus,
and Muslims. I'm sorry to have to return to stress this, but
we could surmount every other obstacle I have mentioned and not
have begun to sense the urgency of it all, unless we face the
fact that although we are not doing more than we should where we

are already working, nevertheless at this time <u>we are hardly</u> <u>even aiming at the major targets.</u>[12] How tragic it is that there is no one place in the world where a number of people with missionary passion are studying in depth any one of the three major targets--the Chinese, the Hindus and the Muslims--much less are all three the focus of a major evangelical center. (This is one of the outstanding virtues of the major mission center I mentioned earlier. There for the first time will be a major focus on each of these three in a context in which comparisons in technique of approach can easily be made, rather than for these major target populations to be studied in isolation from each other.) Is it not time we got really serious about breaking through these remaining walls? The virile EFMA-IFMA constituency ought to have 1,000 people specializing in each of these three areas. Not handfuls. Not a furloughed missionary here or there on secular campuses. How can <u>your</u> specific agency respond specifically to this challenge? Where can you personally start?

These deadly dozen obstacles can and must be surmounted for the simple reason that if we continue with missions as usual, that is, missions of the kind and of the scale in which we are now involved, there is simply no possibility of a major new thrust in missions. We must choose this day whether we will hide our eyes from the need and close our ears to the call or whether we will tackle with new decisiveness, mixed with humility and devotion, the unchanging command of a faithful God whose searching heart is still seeking. To hold back now will lead to misery, guilt and failure; the other choice leads through new open doors into the most spectacular mission challenge that any generation in human history has ever faced. If we will awake to new, daring obedience, the future is as bright as the promises of God.

(Note: The author of this paper earnestly welcomes any comments whatsoever concerning the major or minor details of this presentation. Write to the address in Note #10, page 26.

NOTES FOR CHAPTER 1

1. E-2 evangelism is cross-cultural but is able to build on
    some significant point of contact, while E-3 evangelism is
    in a "totally other" situation where there is no overlap
    between the culture of the evangelist and that of the evan-
    gelized. An example of E-2 evangelism would be the attempt
    by Anglo-Americans to win French or Spanish peoples. E-3
    evangelism would be their attempt to win, say, Navajo or
    Chinese or other peoples who have no significant awareness
    of or overlap with the Anglo cultural tradition. These
    categories emphasize going to a foreign culture not a foreign
    country.

2. Both the paper that was circulated in printed form to all
    the participants before the Congress and the paper that was
    given at the Congress are available in the printed compen-
    dium of the Congress, Let the Earth Hear His Voice (World-
    wide Publications, 1975) or as a separate printed booklet
    with an introduction by Dr. Donald McGavran entitled The
    New Macedonia: A Revolutionary New Era in Missions Begins
    (South Pasadena, Calif.: William Carey Library, 1974).

3. It is all too often assumed that a congregation will of its
    own initiative develop efficient E-0 and E-1 outreach. The
    facts are otherwise. Congregations that do are almost
    always either new congregations, highly select in their
    first-generation membership (like the Coral Ridge church)
    or older congregations that have been stimulated from the
    outside by the example of other such churches, or, more
    often, churches that have been goaded and guided by some
    type of "parachurch" mission structure like the Campus
    Crusade Here's Life America program, the Evangelism Explo-
    sion organization established separately from the Coral
    Ridge church, or the Fuller Evangelistic Association's new
    Department of Church Growth, etc. Note then that even E-0
    and E-1 success will likely depend heavily on the evangel-
    istic sodality structures, to borrow a word from cultural
    anthropology.

4. In view of the slight spacial reduction involved in the
    photographic printing of this book, the resulting scale
    is 295 million per square inch or 261 million for a one-
    inch diameter circle. To draw circles using this parti-
    cular scale you may multiply the square root of the popula-
    tion (in millions) by .052. The result will be the dia-
    meter of the desired circle, in decimal fractions of an
    inch. If you need to use a ruler measuring in 8ths or
    16ths. In general, to reduce different-sized populations

to different-sized circles in a single scale you have to take the square root of the various population sizes and <u>then</u> divide by a sufficiently large number to get a convenient set of diameters (or radii). It is handiest of all to use a centimeter scale.

The original, estimated figures from which I have drawn all the diagrams in this paper are as follows. Other estimates will vary slightly but the overall dimensions are all that are crucial to the argument of this paper. See also footnote 5. All statistics are estimates for July, 1977.

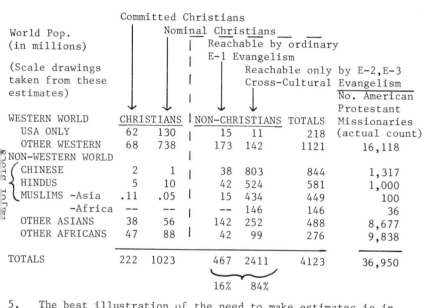

	Committed Christians	Nominal Christians	Reachable by ordinary E-1 Evangelism	Reachable only by E-2,E-3 Cross-Cultural Evangelism	TOTALS	No. American Protestant Missionaries (actual count)
	CHRISTIANS		NON-CHRISTIANS			
WESTERN WORLD						
USA ONLY	62	130	15	11	218	
OTHER WESTERN	68	738	173	142	1121	16,118
NON-WESTERN WORLD						
CHINESE	2	1	38	803	844	1,317
HINDUS	5	10	42	524	581	1,000
MUSLIMS -Asia	.11	.05	15	434	449	100
-Africa	--	--	--	146	146	36
OTHER ASIANS	38	56	142	252	488	8,677
OTHER AFRICANS	47	88	42	99	276	9,838
TOTALS	222	1023	467	2411	4123	36,950

World Pop. (in millions)

(Scale drawings taken from these estimates)

16%   84%

5.   The best illustration of the need to make estimates is in regard to the number of missionaries working in the different areas of the world. The eleventh edition of the Mission Handbook reports the distribution of North American missionaries by continent, but there are estimated to be 7,277 missionaries that were reported in by their boards without a location being given. Thus the figures we have used are the exact number reported in for a given area plus a prorated addition coming from the 7,277. It is not likely that the unknown distribution of the 7,277 is the same as the known distribution of the 29,673 or so properly reported. However a worse error would probably result if the 7,277 were not allocated at all. Thus there are times when any rational estimate is better than none at all. This is the case for many of the numbers in the table above.

6. In a manner analogous to the circle scale, we took the square
    root of the number of missionaries in each category and
    divided by a number that would produce one side of a small
    square of the size desired for our diagram. Specifically,
    there are an estimated 16.965 (thousand) missionaries from
    North America working in the Western world outside of the
    U.S.A. The square root is about 4.12. If we want this
    group to be about 1" square, we can choose simply to divide
    all square roots by, say, 4. This we did. But with the
    additional reduction involved in printing, it is as if we
    were dividing (the square root) by 4.7.

7. The address of the ACMC is Suite 202, 1021 E. Walnut,
    Pasadena, CA   91106.

8. The How and the Why of Third World Missions is a large
    scale analysis of the phenomenon. Readings in Third World
    Missions not only pulls together a wide variety of signi-
    ficant writings on the subject but annotates hundreds of
    other items. Both are published by the William Carey
    Library, 533 Hermosa St., South Pasadena, CA   91030.

9. This superb book is no longer in stock at the original
    publisher--Eerdmans--but is available from the Church Growth
    Book Club, 1705 N. Sierra Bonita, Pasadena, CA 91104.

10. For further information write to the United States Center for
    World Mission, 1605 E. Elizabeth St., Pasadena, CA, 91104,
    Phone (213) 681-7959.

11. Out of print with Eerdmans, available only from the Church
    Growth Book Club, see footnote #9.

12. The table in footnote #4 shows that only 2,575 out of 39,027
    missionaries are associated in any way with the three major
    blocs--that is 6.6% focused on nearly 70% of the non-Christ-
    ians in the whole world.

2
IDENTIFICATION FOR EVANGELIZATION
by Pablo Perez

It is rather difficult to believe that Latin America, with
the largest number of missionaries of any continent, a "highly
religious" population, one of the most influential missionary
radio stations, and but little harassment from its governments
-- to say nothing of its familiarity with Jesus Christ -- can
be considered to be largely unevangelized. It is also rather
sad to recognize that a distance of sorts exists between
national workers and missionary personnel so that their work
towards the urgent need for evangelizing the continent is
affected somewhat significantly.

Yet it is healthy to observe a degree of dissatisfaction
with this state of affairs to the extent that there is a desire
to come to grips with these issues once again so that perhaps
some new steps can be taken to remedy the situation. We should
not forget, however, that these cannot be taken as final solutions, but they are intended to be suggestions along the path
of obedience to the Great Commission. By the same token, we
ought not forget the results of our discussions, nor simply
dismiss them when we find ourselves in disagreement with them,
but rather take them seriously and apply them diligently in our
various fields of ministry. Let us, then, start with some:

BASIC CONSIDERATIONS

Knowing fully well that each generation has to confront its
own problems and attempt to solve them in its own way, it would
nonetheless be good for us to look over the literature, both
recent and somewhat older, concerning joint action for

Pablo Perez, presently President of the Evangelistic Institute of
Mexico, has been a leading pastor in Mexico City, a professor at
Dallas Theological Seminary, and has authored a book on the theol-
ogy of liberation. He holds the Doctor of Missiology from the
Fuller School of World Mission.

evangelization. The amount of material is rather impressive and
its contents quite enlightening and thorough. Yet, to our shame,
it seems that we have profited little from it.

If we look at nothing else but the biblical record, both
in the Book of Acts and the epistles, we find that they unequi-
vocally point to the principle of identification from the very
beginning of the missionary endeavor. The apostles first, then
their followers, and then the rest of the believers considered
themselves to be one with the Spirit of Christ and His objectives, with their particular culture at that particular time in
history, and with one another as true partners in their common
task.

It is important for us to notice that our Lord Himself
established this pattern for what we would now consider a team
where each member becomes both dependable and accountable, when
He presented Himself before the Father to give an account of
the task He had been assigned (John 17, the whole chapter, but
especially v. 4 in this connection). Keeping in mind that this
is an intercessory prayer on behalf of the disciples, we find
that it was also the confrontation of an obedient Son -- as
well as faithful servant -- with the Father and Master who had
sent Him to earth on a special mission with specific aims and
stipulations. On the eve of the consummation of that part of
His mission He reported to the Father that He could be counted
on to fulfill it, thereby showing both the Father and the rest
of the world that He was one with His Father in purpose and
absolute subjection to His will in order to accomplish the one
aim that was all important to the Father: that His name be
glorified.

This, to put it succinctly is the example of identification
at its best: one with the Father in every possible way, as
they had been from before the foundation of the world. Moreover,
as we see from the rest of the chapter, our Lord sought to instill this same attitude in His disciples. As He prayed for
them and committed them to the Father's care, He made sure that
they capture the same perspective before even letting them know
about His command. To Him the Great Compulsion came before the
Great Commission; identification before partnership.

And perhaps we need to capture that same perspective as we
seek to implement the Great Commission as a joint venture. We
will thus discover that it is not the urgent needs or the dis-
tressing circumstances which compel us to evangelize Latin
America, nor the same of a continent that has been declared to
have been "Christianized" over 450 years ago, but the identification with the triune God in His desire to see many Latins turn
to Him.

THE TIME AND SETTING

Missionary history shows us that both the missionaries and the churches they had helped establish had been fully aware of the cultural and temporal aspects of their places of ministry. Our Lord Himself had not ignored the setting where His disciples were to execute His will, and had thus specifically prayed for them in their particular circumstances. It is at this time in Latin America that both the national worker and the missionary need to take a hard look at the circumstances in which they find themselves -- in more than one way.

The previous mission congresses have been but faintly threatened by the specter of the activities of the CIA and its associations with missionaries. I need not go into many of the details as to how this picture has been drastically changed within the last few months, as well as the agony it has produced in many a missionary's heart, without even going into the many unpredictable repercussions.

Just the same, the recent frequent meetings of the so-called "non-aligned nations" have increasingly turned the spotlight on those with whom these countries have close economical and political ties. Uniformity of action -- as in the recent Olympics -- solidarity in spirit -- as in the case of the Panama Canal -- or some type of agreement -- as with the OPEC countries in their price-fixing of oil -- is no more just simply a fad, but a reality that has to be reckoned with and is bound to affect the missionary task in one way or another.

Moreover, the practices of multi-national corporations with their efforts to influence the tides of politics in many countries, and their bribes paid to influential men in government or business, have produced a climate of suspicion toward anything or anyone who may have any connection with a foreign-based or foreign-controlled organization.

It is by now obvious that we cannot simply brush these issues off and hope that they will run their course. We have to face them and evidence both knowledge of the basic problems and an absolute commitment to the Gospel -- as well as an almost unconditional support of the goals and ideals of the land where we minister. This, of course, is no easy task, particularly at a time when there is so much confusion as to the real meaning of terms such as patriotism, nationalism, and some others.

But perhaps the problem is more evident now in Latin
America that the term "liberation" has become highly respectable
and where one cannot even minister properly without at least
mentioning it. Of course, we dare not ignore the many high
and noble ideals comprised in the term; nor can we deny the fact
of the different types of colonialism, imperialism, exploitation
and oppression which are very much a part of every-day life in
Latin America so that social concern is not an issue to be
discussed, but a very necessary task of the church wherever it
may find itself, and to whomever it may be ministering. As we
look at "liberation" we know that we can no longer remain
neutral to its claims and to its effects on the church in Latin
America.

Thus, we need a fuller understanding of the many sides of
the socio/political situation, to be identified with the fact
that "the poor are despoiled" and that "the needy groan" just
as much as God is (Psalm 12:5). Yet again, our identification
should primarily be with the heart of God, with His purposes
and objectives for such adverse circumstances, rather than, as
the popular phrase has it today, "see Christ in the poor."
This calls for discernment and commitment in a somewhat precarious balance.

Still another very important area of our identification
with our surroundings has to do with the main ideological
factor undergirding the life and mind of every Latin American:
Roman Catholic doctrine. It is not simply to delve into the
depths of Thomistic thought or become acquainted with canon law,
but to try to look at life from a Latin American - Roman
Catholic perspective in order to discover many intricacies of
decision-making, discipleship, surrender, and some other aspects
which play an important part in the Christian life.

In all of these issues identification will saturate us
with a knowledge of many angles of Latin American life, and
yet it will not necessarily demand our full participation in
its weaknesses and evils. Our Lord prayed that His disciples
be kept from the evil one while they were still in the world,
and yet He did not pray that they be taken out of the world.
Instead, He prayed for their unity so that the world may come
to know Him.

RELATIONSHIPS

Much has been written about the forms of relationships
that can exist between missionaries and national workers, as
Wade Coggins has recently reminded us.[1] This means that there
have been conscious efforts to work out satisfactory solutions

to a problem that has been a part of the missionary enterprise from early times. Yet, for all of these, we are still wrestling with it and seem to be making little progress to solve it. What can the matter be?

I have already indicated in a previous meeting of EFMA/IFMA that part of the problem is attitudinal, and this involves not only the missionary himself, but the native worker as well. I am also conscious that attitudes are controlled by basic factors which cannot be easily disposed of. There is a need, however, to put them in their proper perspective and to exercise discipline within ourselves in order to keep on correcting them constantly.

On the other hand, we need to examine some of the conditioning factors and the interlocking compartments of our ministries, both of which we usually try to blame for our lack of understanding and full cooperation. This is to say that we are many times chained by our own weaknesses, prejudices, lack of initiative, and super-structures to programs and organizations which literally devour our time and energies but produce little in terms of evangelization. We then tend to blame the type of organization we are under, those who manage it, or even the "constituency" to which we also feel responsible.

Now, while all of the above do play an integral and very important part of our ministry, and while they sometimes can interfere with our task either separately or combined, I would venture to say that most of the times we fall into traps of our own making. This is where we need to discipline ourselves rigorously and not let our hyper-activity delude us into thinking that much is being accomplished.

Just the same, our Board members and the pattern of the structure which they are following, has to be carefully examined. This also goes for the type of government our native churches have adopted, either by their own choice or by the careful teaching of their elders in the faith, whether they are natives or missionaries. This involves not only rules, regulations, and statements of faith, but also the channels used to apply them. In my opinion all of these are in urgent need of a thorough overhauling which will not necessarily follow the example of already existing organizations -- as in the case of the Community of Latin American Evangelical Ministries -- but rather follow the principles behind them and add quite a bit of imagination.

This is because we have to be convinced that unless something bold and fearless is attempted and judgment begins with the household of God, Latin America will remain pretty much the

same way it has for some decades. This in no way is intended
to ignore or demean the personality and sovereignty of the Holy
Spirit. On the contrary, it is an attempt to stop manipulating
Him with our organizations and programs.

But basically, also, it is a desire to foster better relationships among the different members of the same team by trying
to take away as many of the obstacles as possible, relate them
to the basic task in obedience to the Lord, and instill into them
a consuming passion to glorify God through their every effort.
Jesus Christ had told His Father that He had given them the
necessary tools to do the job (John 17:8, 14), and that the key
to conquer the world was that perfect unity evidenced by the
Father and the Son which in turn could be theirs in total
identification.

Here again we find that joint action with the utmost in
effectiveness was not primarily a matter of structures, or plans,
or agreements, but of the bond of unity with the triune God.
Further deepening of relationships that would issue in a strong
partnership was a goal they would have to work very hard to
obtain, but it would at best be one of their aims. Still, we
can say with Charles Troutman, that of all the things we have to
offer to each other, "we can best share ourselves".[2]

STRATEGY

It is becoming increasingly necessary to rediscover this
term both from the perspective of a cybernetic age and of the
ever-contemporary Spirit of God. It has for too long been the
private property of the military, perhaps because of its root
meaning.

Yet we find in John 17 that our Lord is not thinking in
military terms, but He is definitely delineating a bold plan
of action. Having equipped His disciples and given them the
key to win the world, He entrusts them with the task of making
His message of eternal life known. What an audacity! To think
that temperamental James and John would be left in charge of
introducing men and women to Jesus Christ; that unstable Peter
would be asked to feed the sheep; that eternal truth would be
in the hands of a questioning Thomas. But our Lord knew what
kind of a Spirit He could depend on to shape these men into the
kind of servants He needed.

And the Book of Acts is a vivid story of ventures that had
never entered the minds of those simple men. Time after time we
wonder what sense of timing and perception they all seemed to be
possessed by, coupled with unbelievably daring feats which were

at the same time full of common sense. We sometimes have the
idea that because they did those things, and because they are
recorded in the inspired Word of God, there was nothing unusual
about them. But the Holy Spirit lets us look at the way people
reacted to their activities: amazement and bewilderment both
among the believers and unbelievers.

There are, moreover, many and varied ways to evangelize the
whole continent of Latin America if we but make an extra effort
to find them. Let me start by calling to your attention Orlando
Costas' article in The New Face of Evangelicalism, entitled
"Churches in Evangelistic Partnership". Among the many fine
things he brings out in this his commentary on clause 8 of the
Lausanne Covenant, he states some basic considerations which
"can help open the way for a more effective, world-wide, co-op-
erative evangelistic action"[3] as follows:

1. Multiple strategies for varying situations.
2. Multiple ministries for a multi-dimensional task.
3. Multiple forms of evangelistic partnerships.[4]

He then proceeds to explain what each one involves in a way
that is both clear and comprehensive. When he discusses the
third principle he states that:

> partnership does not depend on any form of eccle-
> siastical organization. Rather, it depends on the
> willingness of believers, persons and collectivities
> ecclesiastical and para-ecclesiastical entities, to
> work together for the evangelization of the world
> in concrete human situations through the exercise of
> particular ministries and in accordance with stra-
> tegies designed for these specific ends.[5]

Thus we can focus our attention both on the immensity of
the task and on the wide variety of opportunities open before
us as we attempt to meet specific situations. We could very
easily draw up a list of many of these, but let me just include
a few that have been uppermost in my mind, especially in connection with mass media:

1. A profuse circulation of evangelistic comic books.
2. The use of the soap opera pattern with at least
   three forms in mind:
   a. The television soap opera (called "Tele-novel").
   b. The radio soap opera (called "radio-novel").
   c. The comic book soap opera (called "photo-novel").
3. Public transportation evangelization, both as public
   proclamation and personal work.

4. Beauty shop and barber shop evangelization with
    trained hair dressers and barbers who could also
    evangelize and do quite a bit of counselling.

Again, the above list could grow, but we would do well to
ask ourselves if we have not been so successful in our evangelization that the cults, Roman Catholics, and communists have
copied and perfected many of our techniques so that they are all
now more aggressive in their particular way. Would it hurt if
we recovered some of them and updated them with a stronger
biblical content? If nothing else, it would be worth our time
to look into this possibility.

But in this last area we are in sore need of identification along the lines that have already been presented. Time
after time we see both envy and selfishness which results in
closed lines of communication among ourselves and overprotec-
tion of "our" particular program or idea. On other occasions,
we are willing to share, but up to a certain point, while in
others we are quick to criticize those who, to our way of thinking, are going about the task in the wrong way. It is about
time we identify ourselves with our Lord and cry out with a
loud voice and a heavy groan: "O righteous Father, the world
has not known thee......" (John 17:25). Only then can we hope
to have completed the circle of identification with the triune
God, with our situation, with each other, and with the opportunities before us.

NOTES FOR CHAPTER 2

1. Wade T. Coggins, <u>So That's What Missions is all About?</u> Chicago, Moody Press, 1975, pp. 67-74.

2. Charles Troutman, <u>Everything You Want to Know About the Mission Field, but are Afraid You Won't Learn Until You Get There</u>, Downers Grove, Illinois, 1976, p.33.

3. Orlando Costas, "Churches in Evangelistic Partnership", <u>The New Face of Evangelicalism</u>, C. Rene Padilla, ed., London, Hodder and Stoughton, 1976, p.155.

4. <u>Ibid.</u>, pp. 154-161.

5. <u>Ibid.</u>, p. 158.

3
MISSIONARY ACTION IS AN
"IN-THE-MEANTIME"

by Enrique Guang

I begin these reflections from the basic premise that Paul's missionary work represents one of the most transcendent models for the Third World in the twentieth century. With this thought in mind we will reflect on the preaching-and-teaching nature of missionary work, as well as on the red-hot scene of what today we call the Third World.

As the title of this paper, the writer suggests that *in the meantime* be understood as a concept to be read as: the zeal of the virgins who watched *in the meantime*, waiting for the Bridegroom; as the sense of administrative responsibility of the servants and the talents *in the meantime* while awaiting the return of their Lord; as the rich man's desperate cry in Hades that someone preach to his brothers *in the meantime* while there is opportunity; as a cry for help from people in a burning Third World. It is therefore my desire -- and I feel this burden, brethren of EFMA and IFMA -- that missionary work be understood clearly from the beginning as an *in the meantime* effort.

For this presentation I have chosen to be frank in matters of criticism and simple in presenting suggestions. But criticisms and suggestions have the purpose of contributing to the missionary cause at a time when matters must be handled *in the meantime,* leaving no time for speculation.

I. PAUL'S SCENE AND OURS

If we receive our inspiration from Paul's methods for missionary work, we will find that his scene was much like ours.

Enrique Guang, presently rector of the Alliance Bible Seminary in Guayaquil, Ecuador, has done advanced studies in education, psychology, and theology and is a graduate of the Biblical Seminary of Costa Rica.

Asia Minor, the connecting link between the Near East and Rome,
was a place of great social, economic, and political changes.
It was a land dependent on the Roman Empire. There was religious confusion as a result of Helenistic, Judaistic, and native
thought. There was thirst for liberation and seeking for self-
identity as nations owning their own destiny. Isn't this condition the same as that of the Third World? Yes, it was a first
century "Third World". The difference is that the Gospel advanced in the opposite direction -- from the dependents toward Rome,
and not as happens today with respect to mission centers and
the twentieth century's Third World.

The scene of today's missionary work is a dependent scene
in every form. Economic, technological, education, political,
psychological, and religious dependence are real. A fatigue
at being dependent emerges from this condition, incubating
various forms of rejection and reaction. Fatigue at being dependent -- according to this type of analysis -- would result
from the Third World's not being allowed to find its identity.
It is said that all types of philosophies that speak of liberation find fertile soil here. Add to this the loss of confidence in the stronger one (U.S.) because of what is printed,
said over radio, in TV and movies, etc., about Watergate, the
CIA, Lockheed, etc. And these commentaries (I speak here more
regarding my country) haven't only penetrated the mind of university students, unions, etc., but have also reached the mind
of a sector in the evangelical church which forms part of this
scene. Therefore, when we speak of confrontation between
nationalism and missionary work, it isn't only a secular problem
but also an ecclesiastical problem. Saying it differently,
when Third World people become aware of their poverty and compare European and North American comfort to their own, and state
the needs for economic, agrarian, judicial, social, and educational change in the Third World, this philosophy is already
present in society. But it had made its appearance a long time
ago in the church. When we speak of a red-hot scene, characterized by accelerated change, secularism and paganism, it is a
phenomenon affecting society and church. If a Third World rejection toward any type of vertical treatment from the more
powerful is noticeable, the church also participates in that
feeling in some measure, reaching the extreme in some instances
with national church associations' breaking with the founding
missions. In my country the government published a decree not
allowing parents to give their children English names; only
Spanish or Quichua names are acceptable. It wouldn't be surprising if some sector of the church were to approve this
measure and practice it. Some sectors of the church, especially
youth, have applauded the idea of nationalization of foreign

companies, the capture of tuna fishing boats, etc. And it
wouldn't be strange if they requested national action against
missionary work. In effect, extremist groups have already done
so.

If this is the scene of missionary work, it is imperative
that urgent measures be taken so that the temporal location of
today's missionary and his activity be pertinent to the situation. And as Paul saw clearly the type of scene he was pene-
trating, it is necessary to understand with certainty what the
Third World and missionary activity in it mean. Let's not ever
divorce the work from the scene.

II.   SOME OBSERVATIONS ON TRADITIONAL MISSIONARY WORK
AND SUGGESTED REMEDIES

Critical observations can be made about many things, and
there are ways and purposes for criticism. Due to the limitations of space and time, and because of the objective we intend
to reach, criticism will be measured and pertinent to the theme.
If missionary work is to be considered as a *meantime* activity,
with its meaning of urgency, zeal, and sacrifice, we will give
ourselves to observations and suggestions so that the objective
can be attained. Of necessity, this will bring into question
whether missionary work had had this characteristic or not. Let
us look at a few things so the suggestions are sensible:

A.   *Forever* In Place Of *Meantime*

There is no doubt that there are Third World countries much
like Paradise which invite a person to remain *forever*. They
even become a "second homeland". In the Third World, the missionary force doesn't face great economic pressures, or immediate
superiors, or schedules, or the typical killing way-of-life of
North America. Missionaries can live in the Third World free of
these pressures, they can live happily, being careful to keep up
with reports and correspondence, and a schedule that shows they
are working. But this type of missionary work has little re-
semblance to Paul's model. What we find in his missionary work
is different: he never planned to make the mission field his
forever or his "second homeland". He never lost sight of the
nature of his mission, and he worked with the urgency of the
meantime. I fear that a large percentage of the missionary
force doesn't understand what we are trying to communicate by
meantime.

B.   A Missionary Work That Separates Faith From Understanding Man

In some cases, this area of understanding has been neglected
as a sign of spirituality; in others, as a result of not knowing

the importance of understanding man in the Third World. Missionaries think they know us, but I think they know little of us. Our anthropology, sociology, psychology are a world apart from North America's. And unless an effort is made to know these deeply, missionary work will continue as practiced, as a spontaneous thing from the heart, regardless of results, "as beating the air" (I Cor. 9:26). To know how a man lives, thinks, feels, reacts, why he reacts in a given manner, what values he possesses and how he uses them, isn't contrary to divine leading. Rather, it makes for effective communication of the Gospel, it makes it easier to reach goals, it gives an *in the meantime* urgency to the work. Paul did know the man in the area where he worked and knew how to "become all things to all men, that he might by all means save some." Interpreting this anthropologically, it means to know and identify with people in the area of missionary work.

C. <u>Presenting A Latent and Sterilizing Message.</u>

I begin by explaining the use of terms. The term *sterilizing* is figurative so I fear that the correct idea may not get across. In Spanish the word *castration* has greater meaning, but its use is a bit strong. I am interested in communicating the idea that you can make someone unfruitful, unproductive, sterile -- according to the instruments of communication used. On the other hand, I make a difference between a latent and an overt message in this manner: *overt* is what is verbalized, what is heard; *latent* is that message that need not be verbalized, that doesn't need words, but which is there, which reaches the listener deeply, and has a deeper effect than any form of communication. Now, how can a *latent* message be sterilizing? Here is an example: if a missionary assumes a monopolizing role in the work -- i.e., he teaches, preaches, visits, is musical, is the treasurer-counselor-pastor-evangelist, sings, decides, buys, sells, etc., the *latent* message he is sending to his congregation is: *You are stupid, incapable, inept, don't know how nor are you able, you are the type of people who can't be put in charge of anything.* None of this is said in words, but it isn't necessary to do so, for its sterilizing effects are immediate and mediate. And to prove it, just take a look at the scarcity of leaders in the Third World and the churches that don't produce; they were sterilized at the beginning of their life. If someone were to grade the results of that kind of teaching, it would be *outstanding!* In my judgment as an educator, this may be the worst error committed in missionary work. There has been unfaithfulness to the Pauline principle of discipleship and to the theology of the Body of Christ as a joint work of all its members. And I think this error was made believing that here was the highest indication of *total*

commitment. Comparing our missionary work with Paul's we find
that his wasn't sterilizing. On the contrary, his latent message
was fertilizing, because he stated to his readers that they were
workers together, that they were to follow his example, he
challenged them to wrestle on, showed them they are capable, that
they could and must.....

D. Missionary Work That Still Uses Old Teaching Methods

In part, this is the result of separating faith from human
sciences, and in part, the result of a feeling of self-sufficiency: the idea that the missionary is going to a land of
savages where updated teaching methods aren't so necessary. The
predominant teaching method has been vertical, setting a distance
between the teacher and students, the one who knows and the one
that doesn't, whose extremes are wisdom and ignorance. Because
of this vertical nature, the missionary-teacher is inaccessible
and from this position says, *I know, I can, I decide*. The student is placed on a level where he has to listen, be quiet, repeat, and say: *I don't know, I can't, I musn't*. This is how
sterilization is produced. In other words, in past missionary
work, little has been done about fruitful, horizontal teaching
methods, whether Paul's method of discipling, or the modern
methods used and known in North America (such as Dr. Dale's
"involvement" method, Berne's "transactional" method, the Gestalt
"total perception of reality". In the Third World, and especially
in Latin America, we speak of Paulo Freire's "problem-creating
education", Gutierrez's "total language" method, and others.
In the final section on recomendations, I will provide more
concrete references with examples of what happens when teaching
methods are made more horizontal.

E. A Degrading Attitude Toward The Cultural Heritage of the People of the Third World

An Argentine psychiatrist, oriented toward transactionalism,
affirms: *To degrade is to assassinate; self-degradation is
suicide*. How would we judge the degradation which has been part
of missionary work? In 1916, the Protestant Congress was brave
enough to judge the degrading attitude of its missionary force
by declaring: *We have looked down on the cultural values of the
countries where we work*..... The tragedy is that what was recognized in 1916 did not correct the error, and demeaning attitudes
have continued. This has affected people, submitting them to a
state of sterility, considering them not capable or saintly. It
has affected the evangelical family structure, dismembering it
into a Gospel for women and children, leaving the father out,
who in Third World anthropology constitutes the center of
authority (machismo). It has affected liturgy in that the

legitimate use of our own cultural resources has been denied.
The final result has been that the Gospel hasn't taken deeply
in the family or in certain social strata. It is still looked
upon as a "gringo" religion.

F. The Whole Counsel of God Hasn't Been Declared

Criticism became very strong when the Renovation Movement
appreared with its discipleship program. The Movement judged
that the entire counsel of God hadn't been preached, that the
message had been presented in small "quotas" or "doses". In the
first "quotas", only what the Gospel gives was mentioned. It
was a type of hook to attract people. In the next "quotas" what
the Gospel asks for was gradually added -- not under the Biblical
imperative, but as an option. As a general rule, the peoples of
the Third World learned and received a very easy Gospel. For
that reason the experience of evangelizing, testifying, tithing,
baptism, accepting the call to ministry, is the experience of
only a few persons in the church; the majority are still receiving the first "quotas" (I Cor. 3:1,2). Because Christians
experienced a deficiency in their growth from the beginning,
today we have deformed churches, and no amount of corrective
effort has solved the problem.

G. Mission Fields Considered *a Land of Savages*

I suspect that this problem has been conquered to a point.
But has it? A few years back the principal objects of photo-
graphs weren't the beautiful and well-developed areas we have,
but the most savage parts and our poverty. The image of a
savage Third World seems to be present in the mind of the
sending churches here. In my judgement this has brought on the
following problems:

1. The missionary goes to the field as though to domesti-
cate the people and change their culture, all of which takes
away energy and time from his preaching ministry. The criticism one hears regarding this is very disagreeable. The
people begin to confuse the missionary with some type of
agent for cultural change.

2. The Third World, seen as a land of savages, doesn't
constitute a challenge or an incentive to a more adequate
orientation of the missionary's method and message.

3. There has been a careless abandonment of the great student world and also of the professionals that make up the
middle class. Psychologically, the missionary hasn't been
prepared to work at this level, because he was under the

impression that he was coming to a world of savages. Therefore, we received a Gospel for the poor and ignorant and a
predominantly poor church developed.

The question now is, with all this criticism, what solutions
are proposed? Let's look at some concrete suggestions as
contributions to the future work of the missionary force,
with the sincere hope that work in the future will bring
great success, taking maximum advantage of the *meantime*
period opportunity remaining.

III.   CONTRIBUTIONS TO FUTURE MISSIONARY WORK

We have gone only as far with our criticism as we are able
to contribute suggestions. What is offered in this section is
the result of two decades of direct observation of missionary
work, as an objective observer and as a short-term missionary.
It is the result, also, of commitment to the work as a Latin
American and as a servant of God.

A.   That Objectives With Immediate Priority Be Established Dis-criminating From The Mediate

To discriminate between objectives is a sign of maturity.
And no one should be blind to the real fact that rapid and radical changes are occurring in the Third World. We have the example of Indochina, which could easily be repeated tomorrow in
Latin America. *In the meantime*, while doors are open, let's
determine priority objectives for missionary work:

1. I suggest that every effort be made for dynamic and
practical theological education to produce national leaders
who, in a short time, can take charge of the ministry and the
leadership of the work. If missions should have to pull
out, a trained corps of national leaders would be evidence
of their having followed Paul's method.

2. I suggest that churches be planted in urban centers and
among controlling social classes where there are human and
economic resources, so that the church is able to survive
any change, projecting itself as a missionary church. The
mission today must take charge of the immediate and the
church will be able to perform the mediate. We have produced
many rural churches, poor and small; let's produce another
type of church as an immediate task.

3. I suggest that the methodology of missionary work be
revised, but I will bring this up later.

4. I suggest that the missionary be better prepared to
understand Third World man, his culture, psychology, etc.
This involves the responsibility of suggesting and requesting radical change in curriculum and methodology in theological education centers where missionaries are trained (i.e.,
an open education that includes field experience in the Third
World). Time is short, so with an adequate understanding
of Third World culture, the Gospel can be communicated more
effectively. In seeking to establish objectives one should
take into account culture and present history -- then clear,
simple, and attainable objectives would inevitably emerge.
What a person wants or is able to do would no longer be the
norm, but what must be done.

B. That Missionaries Be Trained to Use a Fertilizing Teaching
    Method

Brazilian pedagogue Paulo Freire speaks of the need to
convert the teacher in explaining the need to change teaching
methods from the vertical to the horizontal. I would say, *the
need to change methods used by the missionary*. This point alone
demands a separate paper because of the transcendence and extension it represents. But because of limited space and time, I
will offer a basic, conceptual outline. The horizontal aspect
of new teaching methods in missionary work should include the
following:

1. To recognize, as Carl Rodgers teaches, man's capacity
    (in this case Third World man) to develop and correct him-
    self, his teacher helping as an adviser. The process cen-
    ters in the student and not in the teacher, so that the
    student develops himself. This would guarantee the forma-
    tion of leadership that the Third World needs. This change,
    more in attitude than method will remove the excessively
    directive role of the missionary and give place to the de-
    veloping national leader.

2. To make of Third World man the subject who carries out
    work in the context of ministry, rather than the passive
    receiving object of the missionary's work. If he is assign-
    ed the role of an active subject, he will be fertilized; but
    if he is treated as a passive object, he will be made sterile.
    This means that from the beginning, responsibility will be
    delegated and work will be decentralized. It will demon-
    strate that there is confidence in his capabilities. The
    disciple will make many mistakes, but the only way to learn
    is by doing.

3. To involve the people of God, in all phases of life,
seriously and really in the work of the Church. We speak,
therefore, of a *change of method* for older Christians, but
we also speak of a new atmosphere to be discovered by younger Christians. The knowledge of God won't be according to
Greek categories or at the level of the mind but according
to the scriptural pattern that means real, active, live
experience. The Third World Christian will be a better
Christian if he is involved concretely and with all his
senses in Christ's cause. And this, which is true in Dale's
secular involvement pedagogy, is really true in the teaching
function of the church by its own nature and theology.

4. To establish the horizontal relationship between missionary and man in the Third World -- where any attitude of
omnipotence on the part of the one or the other should have
been resolved -- that will of necessity make transaction
easier, according to Berne's teaching. Transaction here
means the mutual transfer of content from one to the other;
it is the transformation of those who align horizontally.
And this teaching from Berne's transactional school was first
a reality in Christ's and Paul's discipling practices. A
horizontal position to achieve transaction is more an attitude than a method. But the urgency of missionary work, as
well as the nature of Biblical discipleship, demand change,
even when this means sacrifice, resignation, surrender.
Transactional pedagogy demands the horizontal by the simple
fact that there is no transforming influence where there
is dependence; only where there is liberty, choice, equality,
and brotherhood.

5. Future missionary pedagogy must be social. It isn't
possible today to continue accepting old sociological
theories, such as *man alone* made to live alone. Nor can we
accept the theory of *mass man* where individuality dis-
appears. We accept the reality of man as a social being,
who maintains his individuality, yet functions in society.
In this manner the group forms or deforms the individual;
it heals or makes him sick. The individual away from the
group becomes dehumanized; and as a fact, mental illness
appears in its multiplied ways when an individual separates
from the group. Also, separation is a sign of illness.
Taking this to the Christian level, and concretely to
missionary work, may our labors never break bonds, isolate
individuals, or bring on illness in individuals due to
isolation. On the contrary, may our Gospel go to the family
group as to a microsociety so that it reaches the community
as an enterprise of faith. When we say something, let us
say it as a group; when we do something, let's do it as a

group. Let's demonstrate that the community of faith called the church is a body -- the Body of Christ -- where members work unitedly (Eph. 4:11-16). When we bring new people into the church, let us make every effort to bring them as a total family. We have evangelized individuals too long, we have isolated them, and as a result, we have sick churches made up of separated individuals.

6. The pedagogy of today's missionary work must be based on an integral perception of Third World man (how he lives, thinks, reacts, believes, holds, etc.) as well as on teaching a total Gospel (not only offering salvation, but giving the Gospel's demands -- in other words, the entire counsel of God). We affirm that his manner of understanding reality integrally is God's *gestalt* revealed in the Gospel. Therefore, by integral perception of Third World man, we mean to recognize poor and rich, rightists and leftists, men, women, and children (the tendency has been to evangelize the poor, those of the right, and mainly women and children). Let's see people, and not only souls; let's see people with their cultural heritage, framed within a particular history, sociology and psychology . . . and not displaced from their real life. With this kind of *gestalt* we will obtain a different church.

C. The Transfer of Leadership, Properties, and Autonomy

The evidence that missionary work has been carried on as *in the meantime* will be demonstrated by various forms of leadership being placed in national hands very early. Some denominations have turned over the leadership of some things only when laws have been enacted demanding that nationals administrate offices, schools, or preside. The best reason for turning over leadership should be the aspiration of seeing a mature church. Some denominations have sensed the importance of turning over the titles of properties to the national church making it responsible for this administration. The ideal is to permit gradual autonomy as a sign of *coming of age*. The idea of transferring leadership and autonomy corresponds to the Biblical teaching that a church, having begun under the mission, becomes autonomous and missionary. In Paul's missionary work, typified by short stays in each place, we find the model for today's missionary work: not to remain dominating the scene *forever* but *in the meantime,* while the church is being formed.

D. Reevaluate the Third World's Cultural Heritage

This has been dealt with in many congresses, consultations, etc., yet it continues to be an unresolved problem. I don't

think it has an easy solution, especially when it implies changes
in the cultural structure and reference of the missionary. It
is noted that missionary children give greater value to Third
World culture because of having been born there or lived there.
The problem becomes serious when we note that the first generation of Third World Christians was taught to think poorly of its
culture. For example, it is believed that imported hymnology is
sacred, but what arises from our folklore is pagan, secular, and
to be thrown out. "The people learned their lesson well." But
there is a new moment in the Third World church that must be well
understood by missionary forces -- it is the moment of the self-
identity of God's people as a Third World people. Let me indicate two events that took place in my country in July. There
were two festivals of evangelical song. I attended the first
one in Guayaquil. There were 43 musical presentations, of which
only three numbers were taken from the formal hymnbook. The
rest represented folklore from the three Americas and some from
Africa. The other festival took place in Colta in an Indian
framework. In this festival Andean and Pampa folklore dominated
100 percent. Participants in both festivals came from Argentina,
Chile, Peru, Eduador, Bolivia, Colombia, Venezuela, and Panama.
Apart from the three numbers taken from the classic hymnal, there
was no other imported hymnology. The absence of missionaries
was also noticeable. Was it because it was so pagan? Is it
that missionary forces will never give any value to our culture?
Isn't this a demonstration that the intention was *forever* even
in music? Almost a century has passed and just now God's people
are beginning to express themselves in their structures and
categories, beginning to give value to their anthropology. And
as Galileo, who could stop speaking about the earth's movements
and shape but couldn't stop it from moving, so also the missionary body should not and cannot stop the historical development
of the mission fields. On the contrary, the work of the
missionary in relation to this cultural problem must be to bring
value to it. At the university where I study, there are great
signs announcing a Latin American festival of song and poetry.
A subtitle reads *"campaign against cultural imperialism"*. When
I think of missionary work, I wonder if it isn't confused with
what the Third World is refusing.

When speaking of giving new value, I believe there is folklore -- an instrumentality that is good and can be rescued for
God's glory. It isn't a matter of syncretism or adjustments to
the Gospel, but rather to allow people expression in their own
manner, to communicate their own mental and linguistic structures,
etc. It is a matter of giving people and their cultural heritage their proper worth.

IV. CONTRIBUTION OF PRACTICAL EXAMPLES IN
HORIZONTAL MISSIONARY WORK

Many may say that what has been stated up to now is utopia, theory, or idealism. For that reason I want to offer a few examples of what happens when missionary work has a different orientation. A doubt in another's mind might be "Is it possible to change everything by just applying what has been suggested here?" The answer is "yes", since what is suggested is only a reinterpretation of the divine method revealed in His Word and applied to the growth of the church. The only thing we have done is to read it through a modern semantic, in agreement with the twentieth century; yet its principles were in the Bible from the beginning. When we begin obeying God again, He will bless His work; for when He made the plan for saving the world, He chose all His people to be witnesses, He declared that each Christian is light and salt of the earth that they be fruitful, etc.

Let us see some examples, beginning in this your land:

A. The Coral Ridge Experience

It is well known to you so I will be brief. It is the change that took place in a church where the action centered around Pastor Kennedy (vertical method), to a church where work is shared among all members (horizontal method). It grew from 30 to 2,000 members. The first thing done was to recognize that according to the nature of the church, God was not being served. There was admission of sterility in the church due to vertical methods. The task was made horizontal through discipling, and the entire panorama changed as a result. They began to work according to the plan God established for His Church. And this example, though not from the foreign mission field, contains the same principles that will work in the Third World.

B. The Experience of *Lima Towards an Encounter with God*

In another context and with another people, as long as the same principles are followed, the results will be the same. The development of the Lima Alliance Church, which started this program, has seen growth from 150 to 1,000 members in about two years. The same as with the previous case, the first step was to recognize that the work had been carried on out of step with Biblical principles and the nature of the Church of Christ, so the following project was put into action:

1. Prayer cells at church and in homes praying for wisdom and divine power.

2. The goal: to reach more people, especially those with greater resources (middle class).

3. Training members for evangelism, counselling and all forms of service.

4. Construction of a large church building, adequate for the number of persons to be reached.

5. House-to-house evangelism and visitation before and during campaigns.

6. Preparation and distribution of literature geared to the culture and level of people, both in content and presentation.

7. A 16-month campaign -- each month, 15 days for evangelism, than 15 days to edify new believers, preparing them for baptism and testimony.

8. Simultaneous instruction for the church through the Bible Academy.

9. Projecting an evangelistic program to new areas using a trained congregation, providing a greater challenge, resulting in new churches.

10. Solid planning to repeat the experience in daughter churches, with the same marvelous results.

The results up to now: a large church, with unbelievable human and material resources, with missionary vision and responsibility in the task. In other words, a fertilizing church. (More information may be obtained from The Christian and Missionary Alliance.)

C. The Experience in Colta, Ecuador

This is the old kingdom of the Puruha Indians of the Ecuadorian Andes, the greatest concentration of Indians in the nation. It is totally different in context and ethnology to the previous cases. Poverty, exploitation, slave traffic, etc., are the bread of every day. Several denominations failed in their efforts to evangelize through schools, clinics, radio stations. In my opinion, the reasons for failure were the vertical and aculturating forms of evangelizing. A group of young missionaries from the Gospel Missionary Union discovered the secret: "The task must be made horizontal, because adequate evangelism can only come through the members of the tribe." Here again the Biblical principle was appearing. Training courses -- house-house, and to the community -- were put into action, in their own tongue and through their own people. As a result, the church grew from about 100 to more than 5,000 in about a decade. More than 40 Indian communities have local congregations now. It is the only Ecuadorian church that could be called truly missionary, as they have sent and supported preachers who in turn have started several churches in Southern Colombia. They sought out Indians who migrated to the cities: and in Guayaquil, they formed a church of 300 members in less than a year. (For more information, I recommend Jacob Peter Klassen's thesis, "Fire on the Paramo, a New Day in Quichua Receptivity," 1975 School of World Mission and Institute of Church Growth, Fuller Theological Seminary. There you find an analysis of what happened in Colta along with statistical data, previous and present history.)

D. The Experience in Otavalo, Ecuador

This is very similar to the previous case, but it is more recent and in full development. These are an Indian people who are very proud of their race and history. The missionaries' attempts to evangelize from the outside, without being incarnated into Indian anthropology, were ineffective. Who could evangelize from within following an Otavalo structure? There was only one answer: the Otavalo people themselves. Again, the same principles were applied: training of members, teaching them how to evangelize, counseling, urging them on, giving them liberty to evangelize in their own manner, forming their own liturgy and hymnology, using their own instruments, setting up their form of government. The results: up to 165 percent growth a year.

I could continue quoting experiences, like the Salasaca and others, but I believe this is sufficient. Other parts of the Third World have similar stories. Cultures, times, and missions may vary; but divine principles transcend space and time.

V. A SUMMARY AND A CHALLENGE

Other speakers will focus on evangelism, administration, missionary presence or absence, relationship between missions, etc. I purposely haven't touched on these, concentrating on the methodological and anthropological problem, using Paul's missionary work as a model and the theology of the work of the Church as a Body as the directing criteria, with all its implications and possibilities. I have avoided elaborate formulas because I believe them to be circumstantial. I have preferred to call attention to more transcendental principles. For example, I have not spoken of campaign formulas, but rather of

the Biblical principles of involving the entire congregation;
and if campaigns are planned by a church, they be carried out in
the atmosphere of body commitment. To commit the entire church
you need a fertilizing method, and in this paper we have made
only superficial reference to method.

Putting it all together, we have the challenge to change
attitudes and methods -- a thing that must happen to individual
missionaries as well as in the working philosophy of missions'
headquarters. And above all, if we understand missionary work
to be *in the meantime* -- urgent and serious, with the anguishing
spirit of an Abraham seeing God's wrath falling on Sodom and
Gomorrah -- every effort will be put forth to know the Third
World man who needs to be redeemed. And methods will be changed
to follow the principles of the Word. And when the *meantime* of
missions comes to an end, may the Third World have a church that
is holy, strong, and missionary. Amen.

4
NEW PATTERNS FOR THE FUTURE

by Wade T. Coggins

Some long established patterns in missionary activity are beginning to feel the strain of an increasingly complex world. Rapid changes in the world do not allow us the luxury of leaving our methods unchanged and unchallenged. True, we are committed to the unchanging Word of God. It is our authority and we willingly submit ourselves to its discipline. There are many changes in procedures and methods, however, which could draw us more in line with the Bible rather than moving us away from it.

Many patterns are anchored more in tradition and history than in the Word of God. This paper will explore the possibility of change in some areas of our work and ministry.

Today's situation calls for missionary personnel to be more closely related to and aligned with the local people where they serve. This includes a close relationship with the existing church, greater depth in understanding of the culture, and the development of deep roots within the nation of ministry.

A number of factors make this increasingly possible. Good anthropological courses for the missionary in preparation make him more aware of the need for this and also aware of ways to accomplish it. The already established churches give a body within the new culture which can interpret culture to the missionary who serves there. This emphasis on closeness and depth of understanding is valid and must be taken into consideration in forming our patterns in the future of missions.

Wade T. Coggins, presently Executive Director of the Evangelical Foreign Mission Association, was for six years a missionary in Colombia with the Christian and Missionary Alliance and also for some time a pastor in the U.S. He is a graduate of Nyack College and has an M.A. from the University of Maryland. He has written extensively and is widely known as the editor of the Missionary News Service Bulletin and the author of the recent *So That's What Missions is All About*.

Currently with the concept of deeper understanding and closer involvement comes the call for <u>mobility</u> of the missionary force. Mobility requires structures allowing for rapid movement of people from one place to another. This also is technically and physically more possible today because of rapid transportation and other factors favorable to mobility. Furthermore, it is common in the secular world around us for people to move not only from one place to another but from one career to another. Consequently, mobility is an accepted way of life and has proved itself effective in many ways.

There are factors in the world situation which support the idea of more flexibility and mobility. For example, in many countries it is possible to secure a visa for a short term of three to six months of ministry, whereas it would be difficult to obtain a traditional residence visa.

The availibility of people also makes this option attractive. More people are offering themselves for various types of short term service. A recent survey among EFMA missions indicates that about 10% of the current missionary force is involved in a term of service of two years or less. If missions develop patterns conducive to this type of service, it is likely that more resource people will become available in the future.

The <u>need</u> for development of <u>specialized</u> areas of ministry also makes the concept of mobility and flexibility attractive in today's world.

When an overseas church, for example, decides to put on a stewardship drive among its members it is feasible to bring from another country a person who has been trained and experienced in stewardship to meet with pastors and committees and develop a program which could be applied within that local church.

Such teams of specialists may have an excellent ministry in many different places on a short term basis.

The call for <u>deeper</u> <u>understanding</u> and <u>commitment</u>, and the call for <u>mobility</u> and <u>flexibility</u> seem incompatible at first glance. How is it possible, we ask ourselves, to obtain the in-depth cultural understanding that seems desirable, while at the same time developing mobility, which presupposes people who will stay for a short period of time.

One answer to this paradox could be the development of service at two levels, each of which would meet one aspect of the dilemma.

This concept presupposes the development of a core of leadership from the national church providing guidance in the missionary endeavor. To this core could be added missionaries who will study the culture and language and become a part of the local team on a continuing basis.

There are two ways in which this could develop. Doubtless the ideal would be for greatly strengthened evangelical fellowships to serve this function for a number of cooperating churches and missions.

In the absence of such a fellowship, it may be possible for a national church and a mission to work out a modified form of this same concept.

In either event, the local core of church leaders and resident missionaries would maintain intimate contact with the local situation and the needs of the churches. It could serve as a clearinghouse for many activities, scheduling seminars and training events to avoid overlap and duplication.

It could arrange for seminars that would deal with a wide variety of matters where the church needs specialized help in developing programs and working toward its goals. The core group could bring teams for pastors conferences, for church growth seminars, for missions seminars, and for seminars dealing with education, medical service, literature, and any number of other specialties. This could help greatly in bringing the activities of para-church groups into the mainstream of church life.

The mobility and flexibility aspect of our concern would be met by a growing pool of people trained and experienced in the various specialties which might be needed. These could be made up for the occasion or could be established in regions of the world to reduce the need for long distance travel. This would provide an opportunity to develop international teams made up of people from Europe, North America, Asia, Latin America, or Africa. These international teams would provide their services for study courses of three to six months or short seminars as the individual case might demand. Where conditions permit, the program could include involvement in research centers and graduate schools of theology and missions.

The parallel development of core groups at the location of ministry and international teams to meet the felt needs would require a great deal of commitment, prayer and planning on the part of all. It would also require a greatly strengthened fellowship movement around the world to provide the cooperative core groups which are essential to this concept.

At the location of ministry, mission and church would have to dedicate personnel and money to the development of a strong office with the needed staff to operate its programs. The role of the core group or fellowship would be to ascertain the needs and desires of the local church body and plan the needed programs. A request would then go out to other nations for the needed personnel.

Development of such a program would require significant changes in our traditional outlook and programs.

In developing the international teams there are two approaches which might be used simultaneously to initiate some preliminary steps. In fact, a few faltering steps have been taken. Take, for example, the work of CAMEO (a joint committee of IFMA-EFMA). CAMEO has on several occasions recruited teams to go around the world and talk about Theological Education by Extension. These teams held seminars and informed people about the concept of TEE. From those trips around the world interest grew and in many places programs have sprung up.

This same type of work could be done by other joint committees, which in the future could be based in other parts of the world and draw not just upon North American and European churches but upon the experience which has developed among the churches of Asia, Africa and Latin America.

In another CAMEO project, the Conservative Baptist Foreign Mission Society loaned to CAMEO a person trained in the techniques of writing programmed materials for theological education by extension. Dr. Lois McKinney was assigned to Brazil, where she was invited by 18 training institutions as a resource person and has been involved in training Brazilians in the techniques of developing TEE programs and of writing programmed books. Forty-four interns have participated in the program. Dr. McKinney is serving there to meet a specific need and has developed a core of Brazilians who are trained in the whole matter of extension education and are developing materials for it. New books are being produced at the rate of one or two per month. This lays the groundwork for a future time when Brazilians may form part of a team to go elsewhere and help develop a similar program in other nations.

We should not wait until some great, spectacular worldwide program can be developed. Instead, we should watch for opportunities for developing on a small scale such programs as we have been illustrating here. These will begin to build. Out of them will grow new trained people and new interest. These would form the basis for development of international teams.

One other example along the same line is the work of the joint committee, Evangelical Missions Information Service. Dr. Vergil Gerber, under its auspices, has been very effective in church growth seminars in many parts of the world. Here again, a local committee, frequently the evangelical fellowship, forms the core group. Sensing the needs of the churches and knowing the local culture and language, it forms the nucleus to invite the team. The team then comes in to present the material. Frequently, local church leaders join the team in a given country. In many places local committees have then produced variations of the program for use in their country. They carry forward the concepts, applying them to their churches or denominations.

These developments certainly should anticipate the day when training and research centers will be started in various parts of the world, so that teams would not always emanate from the "West". At such centers it would be possible for people to receive preparation for their service within the general area of culture where they will serve.

From that experience will come the growing internationalization of a strike force of the church which can move into opportunities all around the world to take advantage of openness and receptivity whenever they occur.

A new factor which can tie in with this development is the growth of Third World missions. Missionaries coming from Africa, Asia and Latin America can supply a new dimension to the potential force to meet the requests of churches in a given region of the world.

Recognizing the importance of consultation among missions now developing in Asia, Africa and Latin America and the older missions from the "West", a meeting of the general secretaries of existing evangelical associations of missions has been set for next January in India. It will establish lines of communications and can perhaps contribute to the stimulation of missionary concern in the churches around the world. It will be a small working conference of some 15 individuals. It may be able to begin steps toward coordination of the missionary concerns of the western churches and those now established in all parts of the world.

The development of a missions program in local churches around the world calls for many changes. Local churches must seek ways to stimulate prayer for missions, to provide guidance to young people who will become missionaries, and to lead the people into missionary giving. Simultaneously, missionary training programs must be developed either within the existing training institutions or in addition to them.

While at the threshold of a new era, it is urgent that we allow the Holy Spirit to teach us new patterns to meet the unprecedented needs of our times.

I want to touch on (without really developing) some additional areas where pressures are calling for changing patterns. Some may tie in with the concepts of the earlier part of this paper, while others will develop separately.

New patterns are developing in the area of church-mission relationship. These may serve as a transition from older methods to the pattern suggested in the early part of this paper.

From the point of view of both denominational and interdenominational missions, new patterns are needed. We have dealt with this issue in past consultations, but it continues to be a matter of critical importance. It is essential to find ways to allow maximum participation by the maturing church in the planning and development of programs sponsored by the mission.

The development of written agreements or contracts between the mission and the church is helping to accomplish this in a number of places.

This procedure allows maximum opportunity for input from the national church leadership as they sit down with the mission representatives for an extended time of interaction and discussion. They work through an agreement which involves setting goals and developing programs for a specified period of time. After planning a strategy for outreach and ministry, together they determine the resources (of personnel and money) needed to accomplish the goals. The mission tells what it will be able to provide and the church determines what it can provide.

The resulting agreement will state the goals and objectives of the program under discussion. It will describe the types of workers needed and will provide job descriptions for the individuals to be requested from the mission. It will also outline the plan for financing the project. The agreement should also state methods of supervision of the work and a system for evaluating the performance of the mission personnel.

The responding mission is then called upon to screen candidates in view of the request, and to work on agreed upon long-range financing. Preliminary training is given to the staff who will be sent.

Such agreements have a very valid role to play, because they provide for specific input from the church and its involvement in the decision-making process. The missionary appointed under this system understands what his work is and he knows that it is wanted by the church. He can enter into it with enthusiasm and full involvement.

For some groups which are not yet using this system a real problem has developed with regard to the missionary morale. When missionaries are sent out to the field without a clear definition of what they are going to do, frequently they begin to feel a sense of frustration when they see the mature national church with its own strong program. Clear instructions from the church through written agreements will certainly help to overcome this particular problem, making clear to the missionary where he fits into the picture.

Theological Education by Extension is a new pattern of missionary work which promises to have an important impact in the next few years. The term TEE is used to describe an extremely wide variety of education effort around the world. An enormous effort by national leaders and missionaries is being poured into TEE programs.

Dr. Lois McKinney estimates that from 1974 to the present time she, the 44 Brazilian interns and their mentors have invested 35,840 hours into the program. Based on a 40-hour work-week without vacation, that is the equivalent of more than 17 years of work poured into the project in its years of operation. Multiply this by the scores of programs in process around the world and it becomes evident that this movement is a major new pattern which will continue to have an increasing impact in the coming years.

Dr. Wayne C. Weld, who edits a paper called "Extension", estimates that there are 250 programs of TEE located in 40 countries, with some 30,000 students enrolled.

The possibility of using research effectively to improve Gospel outreach is gaining acceptance among the missionary community.

Elements of research are found in the teaching of Church Growth as developed by Dr. Donald McGavran and as applied by him and many others. The concept involves the use of the skills of anthropology and sociology to understand people and approach them in a way that will gain a positive response.

For a number of years MARC (a division of World Vision) has been developing research techniques and materials which provide valuable help to those involved in missions.

A more recent strand in this growing awareness of research and its value to missions comes from the Wheaton Graduate School of Communications. Techniques for "audience" research are being developed and taught. Such research helps to identify where people are in their spiritual awareness. The message is then aimed to challenge them to move toward a greater awareness and finally to a decision.

It appears that the use of research methods will increase over the coming years as it becomes more evident that those using it do not retreat from their recognition that God does the work of regeneration in men's hearts.

The practical application of research is being demonstrated in actual field experience. In 1975, for example, a task force in Central Nigeria studied a region involving some 30 tribal groups. The purpose of the research was fourfold: to identify and describe the various unevangelized peoples of Central Nigeria, to expose the need of these target groups before the church body of Nigeria, to point out factors that have hindered (or encouraged) evangelism in these groups, and to suggest a strategy that is culturally related and one that will enable the church in Nigeria to grapple realistically with the completion of the task.

After one phase of the study, a Nigerian member of the research team reported finding a very open group. He recommended to the Nigerian church that they immediately send 100 workers. Each worker would live in a "household village" and plant a church. This is research geared to action. (For details see AFRICA PULSE, August 1976.)

Efforts to involve American Christians from the business and professional community have not been widely successful in the past. There have been, of course, isolated cases of exceptional fruitfulness through involvement by people in that category.

Some special efforts by missions are being made to provide for their effective involvement. International Christian Fellowship is one of several missions which is having a specfic program designed for them. ICF calls the program the "Field Partners Scheme." It is designed to establish a link to the mission for Christians involved in any kind of overseas work. Field Partners are not connected contractually and no financial link exists. Partners are expected to be in sympathy with aims, work and doctrinal position of the mission. They will be involved with missionaries in prayer, mutual encouragement, and practical help where possible.

It is estimated that there are some 100 Americans working overseas for each missionary. Within that group are numerous Christians who would like to find closer ties to the mission and church. It is a pattern which needs to be explored.

In the field of Communications there is a need for developing new patterns of cooperation and coordination. Specialized communications ministries need to draw closer to the churches, and new modes of cooperation among communications need to be developed.

Some agencies involved in recording, cassettes, and other types of special ministries have recently met to discuss common strategies. This is an important step in the right direction.

Project Look-Up is a cooperative effort to secure broadcast time for television on an educational satellite. If this develops it will set a new pattern.

I will close with brief comments on a few additional likely patterns which need further study and evaluation in the future.

The practice of missionaries coming on a long vacation (2 or 3 months) every second year instead of being uprooted for "furlough" every four years will probably increase in coming years as various problems in the system are resolved.

The deployment of personnel through a second missionary society instead of beginning a whole new operation is a concept which is being used to some extent as a new pattern. Actually, it is a very old pattern, but it has not been widely used. Some are rediscovering it today as an alternative to starting another "denomination" where a number of evangelical groups already exist.

The practice of "loaning" personnel to special projects of a cooperative nature will increase. There is increasing demand for such people in programs related to TEE, Church Growth, graduate level training, fellowships, literature projects, and other cooperative efforts.

The "Rosario Plan" of evangelizing the city of Rosario, Argentina is an example of churches and missions pooling their efforts for a strong, dynamic outreach. Brother Luis Palau will be telling more about this on Thursday night. Other possibilities along this line should be explored.

Another pattern which should be explored is the development of ministries which can be income producing, enabling

them to function with less foreign money. Christian Literature
Crusade of Fort Washington, Pennsylvania, is an example of this
pattern. They have bookstores which help support local staff
from the sale of books. What are the possibilities in the
fields of language teaching, broadcasting, medical services,
development projects such as agriculture or industry?

There is a desire by local churches to find new patterns
for relating to churches in the regions of the world where they
have supported missionary work that has produced churches which
are now mature. Missions should be listening to this search
for new patterns and providing some innovative thinking in
cooperation with the churches.

Many missions have been responsive to change, developing
new patterns for their work. The pace of change is accelera-
ting, which means that we cannot relax our efforts to do the
best possible job. We must constantly seek patterns which will
meet the needs of the present and prepare us for the future.

5

EVANGELICAL COOPERATION

by Waldron Scott

INTRODUCTION

My visits to national evangelical fellowships around the world are somewhat akin to strolling across the stage during an orchestra's tuning up period. The analogy seems appropriate for several reasons. First, an orchestra, with its essential unity and multiple parts, is certainly an apt metaphor for the global evangelical community. Second, the tuning up process, with each player preoccupied with his own instrument and concerned primarily to perfect his own role, epitomizes the less attractive side of the evangelical world today. Third, there is nevertheless, in the midst of this dissonance, the promise of beautiful music to come. Since I am not a musician I don't want to press this analogy too far. But perhaps it will serve to introduce our subject.

Also by way of introduction let me say that in this paper I do not pretend to discuss all aspects of evangelical cooperation. I only wish to highlight some of the observations I've made and some of the conclusions I've reached during the past couple of years. I'm still learning and look forward to any feedback I may receive from you in response to this paper. Those of you who may be interested in a more comprehensive treatment of this subject are referred to a number of different papers presented at the joint EFMA/IFMA Study Conference of 1973. I presume these papers are on file in the respective IFMA/EFMA offices.

Waldron Scott, presently General Secretary of the World Evangelical Fellowship, was for many years one of the key minds in the Navigators, heading up their work in the Middle East for ten years before becoming Director for Asia and eventually the International Field Director.

EVANGELICALS IN THE MODERN WORLD

Cooperation, of course, is not an exclusively evangelical phenomenon. (Some would say it is hardly an evangelical concern at all!) We see all kinds of cooperative efforts in the world around us: parent-teacher associations, labor unions, political parties, etc. Cooperation at regional and international levels is not uncommon either. During my years of missionary service in Malaysia, ASEAN - The Association of South East Asian Nations, was developed. Its value to participating countries is reflected regularly in the pages of the Far East Economic Review and other publications.

The European Economic Community (EEC) has played a major role in the tremendous recovery Europe has made since World War II, so much so that similar economic unions are being promoted in Latin America, Africa and elsewhere. During the ten years I served in the Middle East, Arab nations believed they were totally at the mercy of a few giant oil corporations backed by the governments of the industrialized world. Only recently have they discovered the power of the cooperative apparatus they helped put together some years back. When acting unitedly through OPEC - The Organization of Energy Producing Countries, they found they possessed the kind of leverage that can bring even the mightiest nations to heel.

One hundred years ago planet earth still seemed very large to its inhabitants. Countries and continents were widely separated. Travel was leisurely, communication sporadic. The population of the world was about one-fourth what it is today. All this has changed. Buckminster Fuller speaks of "spaceship earth", by which he means for us to visualize the smallness and loneliness of our planet. For the first time in history mankind is truly one. Men sense they share a common ecological destiny. They speak of our "global village".

This is not mere sentiment. Modern technology has revolutionized our globe. For the first time ever, through telecommunication and various mass media, all men are in touch with each other. This fact - combined with the population explosion and a new awareness of the limits of shared planetary resources, has created an era of high pressure social change and an unprecedented degree of global interdependence.

In such a turbulent but interdependent world the only units capable of functioning effectively are those which, by virtue of consciously cultivating interlocking resources, achieve sufficient size to withstand contemporary pressures and sufficient

<u>flexibility</u> to adapt to rapid social change. Small units, in so
far as they attempt to operate in relative isolation, are simply
by-passed. They may exist, and even function to their own
satisfaction, but are relatively ineffective and frequently
irrelevant. We see this clearly in the arena of nation-states,
multi-national corporations and international political movements. It is no less true in spiritual enterprises.

Pressures on evangelical communities worldwide are inten-
sifying. The day is approaching when the major forces of the
modern world - nation-states, multi-national corporations,
international political movements - will with few exceptions be
anti-Christian. Evangelicals will also find themselves pres-
sured by the major religious conglomerates headquartered at
Geneva, Rome and elsewhere. These modern religious and secular
forces will possess seemingly unlimited strength precisely
because of their ability to marshal and allocate resources on
a global scale.

Evangelicals, or course, will find their strength in the
Lord. "The weapons we wield are not merely human but divinely
potent to demolish strongholds." (II Corinthians 10:4) Yet
we are not to wield these weapons in uncoordinated fashion. We
are a body - Christ's body - and unless we learn to function
as a body - communicating with each other, dividing our labor,
combining our resources, acting in unity (or at least in
harmony) - our hope of being effective in the modern world will
prove delusory.

I realize I am "preaching to the converted". You are
mission executives. You know that your own agencies have grown
and prospered in direct proportion to your ability to get
recruits, churches, prayer partners, donors, home staff and
field personnel all working together as a team. All successful managers understand this.

So while you have been developing teamwork within your
own mission, IFMA and EFMA, also separately and together, have
been promoting teamwork among missions. Units such as CAMEO
and EMIS (if I understand the situation correctly) are models
of joint action between IFMA and EFMA themselves - as is this
Retreat. Your presence here assumes an awareness of the value
of inter-agency cooperation and some degree of commitment to it.

Nevertheless, while not underestimating our achievements
along these lines, let's be realistic. The truth is, evangelical cooperation - much less real teamwork - is still embryonic.
Christ's team is not really functioning as a team. This is true

in the evangelical community at large, as I have had ample
opportunity to discover these past couple of years. It is
evident also in IFMA/EFMA circles. Why is this?

OBSTACLES TO EVANGELICAL COOPERATION

Numerous reasons are proffered for this state of affairs.
Not all are of equal merit. They range from just plain inertia
to lack of time, from disparate location of headquarters offices
to differences in ministry emphases, from sheer prejudice to
personality conflicts, from lack of finances to doctrinal incom-
patibility.

Of these the matter of doctrine is of special concern to
evangelicals because teamwork presupposes a measure of unity
and for evangelicals unity must be biblically based. Henri
Blocher underscores this in his paper, "The Nature of Biblical
Unity", circulated prior to the Lausanne Congress. "The
possibilities of expressing Christian unity," he says, "are
proportional to the doctrinal agreement reached." Most
evangelicals would agree. Blocher then presents five criteria
for evaluating the relative importance of a doctrinal question
under discussion:

1. The biblical criterion, the place given to the subject
in the Bible itself;
2. The theological criterion, how strategic the doctrine
is;
3. The practical criterion, having to do with the consequence of the doctrine in church life;
4. The historical criterion, how the doctrine has been
evaluated in the past and;
5. The contemporary criterion. "Where men of God,
academically qualified and professing obedience to the Scriptures, find themselves numbered on both sides, we may conclude
that the object of the debate does not belong to this vital
heart of Christianity."

Given the tremendous variety of evangelical experience, and
the complex historical development of our ecclesiastical traditions, there can be no effective teamwork within the body of
Christ without a willingness to make this distinction between
essential doctrines and secondary ones. As Rupertus Melinius
eloquently expressed it, "In essentials, unity; in non-essen-
tials, liberty; in everything, love." Similarly in Philippians
3:15, Paul distinguishes between the fundamental agreement
necessary for two brothers to walk together and the divergen-
cies, even among mature believers, which ought not restrain
the expression of evangelical unity.

(In this connection let me say parenthetically that I expect WEF's International Theological Commission, drawn from six continents and reflecting the major evangelical traditions, to help the worldwide evangelical community maintain its evangelical integrity in the years ahead, and at the same time help us all to address ourselves theologically to the major issues of our day.)

The most obvious and useful implication of all this is that there are several levels of legitimate cooperation. Some evangelicals instinctively assume an either/or posture on every question. All is black and white. Intermediate shades are missing - as if God had never made a rainbow! Yet the ability to discern degrees of cooperative potential and act accordingly is surely one of the requisites of leadership.

In the place of an either/or approach Arthur Glasser suggests five options for evangelicals to consider when deciding on relationships with others. In descending order of intensity these are:

1. total identification
2. active cooperation
3. brotherly fellowship
4. occasional dialogue
5. clear-cut separation

Even with the help of qualifying adjectives the semantics here are not unambiguous. Still, the scale is helpful. It encourages flexibility in acquiring first hand experience with groups unfamiliar to us. It also provides a <u>rationale</u> for maintaining a variety of relationships short of separation.

Doctrine, of course, is not the only factor determining at what level we relate to others. Pablo Perez noted this in his presentation. Variant customs, mores and methodologies often prove decisive. Less excusable are the pride and prejudice born of ignorance. The perceptions implied in Glasser's approach acknowledge this wide range of factors, noble and otherwise, in a sophisticated but biblically consistent way.

The reason I have gone into this in some detail is because the most urgent need that has impressed itself upon me these past two years as I have travelled to most parts of the world - beginning with an initial trip with Clyde Taylor - is the need for "conservative evangelicals", with whom I gladly classify myself, and especially conservative evangelical leaders, to broaden our understanding of the <u>real</u> global evangelical constituency in today's world.

As a result of the modern missionary movement, led in large measure by evangelicals, a truly global evangelical community has emerged. It numbers at least 75 million people on all six continents. This is a conservative figure. There may well be as many as 100 million evangelicals throughout the world. The latest Gallup Poll (August 1976) indicates a startling 34% of all Americans (including half of the country's Protestants) claims to have been "born again". Similar claims, according to the late Byang Kato, are made today by 20 million Africans and millions more in Latin America, Europe and Asia. These "born again" believers cut across all denominational lines. They include Baptists, Lutherans, Pentecostals, Anglicans - even Roman Catholics and Eastern Orthodox.

While it is next to impossible to verify such claims conclusively it is apparent that in the providence of God evangelicals are a significant minority in the modern world. Or, to return to language I was using a moment ago, Christ has a team on earth today, 75 million strong and endowed with able, Spirit-filled men. If Christ's team can come to understand itself as a team, and learn to function as a team, then surely it has the potential to become the greatest force for good in the 20th century.

But will this happen automatically? Hardly! Carl Henry asserts (*Christianity Today*, August 6, 1976) - and I agree - that evangelicals must achieve a larger sense of the evangelical family, "in which fellow believers recognize their common answerability to God in His scripturally given Word, and their responsibility to and for one another."

Henry has replaced my analogy of a team with one of family here, but this intent is the same. Let me speak plainly. The willingness of many conservative evangelical leaders to reach out to this "larger evangelical family" - whether to Pentecostals in Germany, Anglicans in Kenya, Presbyterians in Thailand - and for whatever reasons, remains one of the most complicating factors in evangelical cooperation today.

Because of this reluctance, many of the national evangelical fellowships around the world, with which many of us here would tend to identify, are not really representative of the evangelical communities in their countries. This has serious consequences on the mission field, as we experienced recently with PACLA - The Pan Africa Christian Leadership Assembly. For similar reasons in other parts of the world evangelical cooperation is hindered because of an unhealthy appearance of competition between the Lausanne Committee for World Evangelization

(LCWE) and the World Evangelical Fellowship (WEF). This confusion on the part of grass-roots evangelicals stems directly
from the fact that LCWE is perceived almost everywhere as being
more representative of the true evangelical constituency than
WEF is.

A QUESTION OF WILL

Even when we have settled to our own satisfaction who we
can cooperate with, our actual level of cooperation is generally
low. Why so? Surely this is a question of will, of conviction,
of motivation and - in the final analysis - of vision.

We all acknowledge the New Testament teaching on the body
of Christ. But have we fully understood and embraced its implications? Or have we sometimes drawn faulty conclusions? We
know, for example, that the body does not consist of one member
but of many (I Corinthians 12:14). We know that God arranges
each member in the body as he chooses (I Corinthians 12:18). We
know that Christ is the head of the body (Colossians 1:18) and
that each member is related directly to Him. And we know that
the members of the body all have different functions (Rom. 12:4).

From this we infer, organizationally and denominationally,
that we are essentially "on our own". We assume that if each
of us does "his own thing", looking to the Lord for direction,
then somehow the purposes of God will prevail, the cause of
Christ triumph, and the Great Commission be fulfilled. Unfortunately this overlooks the equally Pauline insistence that as
members of the body we are related not only to Christ but to
each other! We are "individually members one of another"
(Romans 12:5).

Consider some of the implications of this. In the first
place "the manifestation of the Spirit" has been given to each
member not, primarily, for his personal edification or the fulfillment of his agency's mission alone, but "for the common
good" (I Corinthians 12:17). Consequently the members are
supposed to have a common care for one another. "If one member
suffers, all suffer together; if one member is honored, all
rejoice together" (I Corinthians 12:26).

Naturally we apply this teaching within our own societies.
Some missions succeed better than others in so organizing themselves that individual gifts are applied for the common good.
Ways and means are developed to enable members to express their
care and concern for each other. But bear in mind that Paul is
not writing to just one party in the church at Corinth but to
the whole church as a unit - and even beyond Corinth to "all

men everywhere who invoke the name of our Lord Jesus Christ -
both their Lord and ours" (I Corinthians 1:2).

If we apply this today to the larger evangelical community
of which each of our agencies is only a part we must admit forth-
rightly that only a minimum effort is made to coordinate gifts
and ministries for the common good. On the contrary, so preoccupied are we with our own affairs - that is, the affairs of
our mission or denomination - that were Paul on the scene today
he would be compelled to say of us as he did of certain groups
in his own day, "they look after their own interests, not (the
larger interests) of Jesus Christ" (Philippians 2:20).

Now in our day this may be an inevitable expression of
Western individualism. But I think not. The problem antedated
the 20th century. Earlier in his letter to the Philippians,
Paul had found it necessary to exhort, "Let each of you look
not only to his own interests, but also to the interests of
others." (Philippians 2:4) I am amazed at the way some of our
best-known evangelical leaders today interpret cooperation to
mean, "Let's all join together to help my organization accomplish its goals."

Not only are we self-centered; we often see ourselves as
self-sufficient. These may well be the two great evangelical
sins. As with self-centeredness, so self-sufficiency is a
consequence of our failure to embrace the full implications of
membership in the body of Christ. And perhaps, as far as
Americans are concerned, it is also an unacknowledged consequence of our secular membership in history's most affluent
society. Sociologists tell us that any group numbering more
than 100 has a built-in bias toward self-sufficiency.

The New Testament, however, expresses a contrary drive.
It suggests deliberate interdependency. "If the whole body
were an eye," Paul asks, "where would be the hearing?" (I Corinthians 12:17) Again, "The eye cannot say to the hand, 'I
have no need of you.'" (I Corinthians 12:21) Note the word
cannot. The tendency to self-sufficiency is simply contrary
to the intent of God.

Yet within evangelicalism today there is but meager effort
on the part of denominations or societies to express their
biblically compelling need for one another. The Lausanne
Covenant says, "We urge the development of regional and functional cooperation for the furtherance of the church's mission,
for strategic planning, for mutual encouragement, and for the
sharing of resources and experience." (Clause 7) In spite of
this, evangelical leaders continue to look upon cooperative

ventures as a waste of time. When we do come together it is,
more often than not, an expression of convenience - a low
keyed feeling that <u>perhaps</u> there are a few worthwhile ideas to
be exchanged - <u>perhaps</u> a small scale, low budget program worth
supporting.

CONSIDERATIONS FOR THE FUTURE

At this point our African brethren may have something to
teach us. They have learned that evangelical cooperation is
an evolutionary process, a development by stages. They have
identified four distinct stages to the process. They say that:

1. Coming together is a beginning,
2. Staying together is progress,
3. Thinking together is real unity, and
4. Working together is success.

My experience confirms the astuteness of this little outline.
Not only are the four stages separate, they are progressive.
One leads to the next. Furthermore, each stage requires a distinct quantum of input of time and energy and, usually money.
Having expended considerable effort to bring people together for
a project we let them drift away upon its completion. When
another project surfaces later we have to re-invest great quan-
tities of time and energy to start up the machinery again. We
lose the advantage that would have accrued had we stayed together.

One common mistake I observe being made is that of trying
to move directly from the first stage to the fourth.   The
attempt to bypass the second and third stages - staying together
and thinking together - makes our efforts at cooperation less
effective than they might be.

Now it is relatively easy to bring evangelicals together
on an <u>ad hoc</u> basis. And a fair amount of useful work can be
accomplished thereby. One has only to think of the benefits of
a Lausanne Congress or a city-wide evangelistic campaign.
Unfortunately many evangelicals today believe an <u>ad hoc</u> approach
is virtually the only worthwhile avenue to cooperation.   They
feel it is unnecessary to bother with more formal structural
approaches.

Carl Henry, in the article cited earlier, asserts that
the basic evangelical need is not for structural organization
of a para-conciliar sort - that is, the sort implied in stage
2 of the African outline and represented by groups like the
National Association of Evangelicals or the World Evangelical

Fellowship. Henry prefers more informal relationships of the
ad hoc variety, short term responses to particular needs. A
similar preference is expressed by Orlando Costas in The New
Face of Evangelicalism (p. 158).

        This is understandable. Yet wars are not won by "minute
men". They are won by established forces acting jointly to
achieve strategic objectives. In so far as Henry and Costas
are pointing us toward more dynamic ways of spiritual renewal
they are undoubtedly correct. But, as Henry himself points
out, "institutions are indispensable to any movement's dura-
bility, and it is a mark of maturity when evangelicals realize
that institutions must be properly nurtured and cultivated,
and their goals persistently deepened."

        In order for evangelical agencies to act together stra-
tegically over the long term they must become aware of each
other's strengths (and weaknesses) and they must learn to trust
each other. This requires not only coming together but staying
together. And this in turn requires some kind of organizational
framework, however simple. Morgan Derham, Vice-President of
the European Evangelical Alliance, is fond of pointing out that
"communication flows as you pump it, and cooperation flourishes
as you cultivate it."

        Organizations such as IFMA and EFMA and, on another level,
WEF, provide environments for cultivating cooperation on a
sustained basis. But here again evangelicals, fearful lest
such umbrella organizations evolve into Geneva or Vatican -
like bureaucracies - tend to maintain such bodies at a minimal
level. This automatically ensures that stages 3 and 4 of the
African outline - thinking together and working together -
never develop their full potential. As Philip Armstrong of the
Far Eastern Gospel Crusade notes, "Our dislike of ecumenical
over-organization has tied our hands at a time in history when
we should be best able to reach out." (Paper presented at the
1973 IFMA/EFMA joint study conference.)

        Stage 3 is thinking together, the basis for real unity.
"Be firmly joined in unity of mind and thought." (I Corinthians
1:9) Thinking together, in their context, includes praying
and planning and strategizing together. It should be done at
national and regional levels even though this is difficult and
relatively expensive. But thinking together in this way leads
naturally to stage 4, working together, which is success.

        At the local level these activities are comparatively in-
expensive. At their simplest they can be carried off for the
price of a cup of coffee. At the regional and international

levels, however, such activity is costly. But if evangelicals
are to function as a global team - and the historical moment
cries out for us to do so - we must be willing to pay the price.
So far I see little evidence that we are ready to do so. I
live in a medium-size city and belong to a medium-size church.
Yet our congregation, one of a dozen evangelical churches in
our city, has an operating budget <u>ten</u> <u>times</u> greater than either
IFMA or EFMA. Is this not incongruous?

At this point I wish to make two concrete proposals to you
who are related to EFMA/IFMA boards. The first is that you take
positive steps, stronger steps, to help develop and support
cooperative evangelical facilities in the countries in which you
work. My predecessor, Clyde Taylor, believes that the most
strategic level of evangelical cooperation, particularly in the
Third World, is the national level. For my part, I am convinced
that strong national evangelical associations provide the only
viable basis for a more comprehensive continental and global
cooperation - and I have already presented reasons why, in the
modern world, evangelicals should be prepared to act together
at regional and international levels.

If this be so - that strong national cooperative arrangements are essential - then we are in trouble. Some of our
existing national evangelical alliances are strong. But many
are noticeably weak. They lack full time executive secretaries.
They have inadequate offices and budgets.

Surely this is one of the most strategic challenges IFMA
and EFMA face today. It is not enough to evangelize. We have
a responsibility to conserve the fruit of our evangelism. And
that cannot be done by planting churches that live and work in
relative isolation from the rest of the body of Christ. Before
his untimely death Byang Kato, then General Secretary of
AEAM - The Association of Evangelicals of Africa and Madagascar -
reminded us repeatedly that strong national fellowships can save
African churches from an enforced ecumenism.

Radical leaders associated with the World Council of Churches are allocating increasingly large sums of money to develop
and support WCC - related national councils in places as distant
as Korea, Kenya and the Caribbean. Clyde Taylor wryly notes that
"we evangelicals, as soon as we have a slight surplus of funds,
look for another missionary to send out," even though this may
not be the best strategy.

Now I realize and appreciate the fact that IFMA/EFMA
boards were instrumental in establishing AEAM and still support
its Nairobi office. What I wish to point out, however, is that

in today's situation the mere fact of support is not the key
factor. The scale of support is likely to prove decisive in
the contemporary equation. The annual budget of AACC - The
All Africa Conference of Churches - for example, exceeds one
million dollars. Compare that with AEAM's current budget of
$50,000. Is it any wonder that ecumenism gains ground steadily
in sub-saharan Africa?

At the 1973 IFMA/EFMA joint study conference, Milton
Baker of the Conservative Baptist Foreign Mission Society
declared, "It is tragic that so little effort and funds have
been applied to the development of viable, productive (national)
evangelical fellowships. Too often it is only the threat of
some negative force that causes evangelicals to finally 'find'
the funds that could have been used more profitably had they
been designated sooner." Baker went on to propose that EFMA/
IFMA agencies "seriously and prayerfully consider giving at
least one half of one percent of (their) incomes to develop
effective evangelical fellowships worldwide." That was three
years ago. As far as I have been able to ascertain, this
proposal has not been implemented by any IFMA/EFMA board -
though it seems modest enough.

I mentioned two suggestions. The second is that IFMA/EFMA
missions cooperate with WEF in developing stronger relations
with emerging Third World missions. This is one of the chief
purposes of WEF's International Commission on Missions. George
Peters, after making inquiries at a number of Third World
mission offices in Asia, says that the movement may abort.
That would indeed be tragic since the emergence of Third World
missions has been one of the most gratifying phenomena of the
past 25 years and affords great hope for the future.

Leaders of Third World missions and leaders of traditional
Western agencies have much to learn from each other. A crying
need exists for genuine partnership in mission. But the two
groups hardly know each other. And there are but few instances
of working relationships between them. Here again I am convinced that if we evangelicals do not move unitedly and
vigorously in this direction, ecumenical agencies will. And it
does not take much imagination to anticipate what this will
mean to the cause of missions.

Now I am aware of some of the practical problems involved
in my two suggestions. Many IFMA/EFMA boards are structured
along lines of personalized support. This curtails the amount
of money available for allocation through general funds. But
where there is a will there is a way. Moreover, many American

donors, at least, are waiting for mission executives to come up with solutions. Contrary to what we may think American evangelicals are becoming increasingly sophisticated - from a variety of sources - about the needs of Third World churches. They are more than ready, I've discovered, to respond to efforts to involve them in the development of strategic national and regional fellowships.

CONCLUDING REMARKS

Writing in the Spring 1976 issue of Japan Harvest, Siegfried Buss draws attention to the Japanese (*kanji*) word for cooperation. Transliterated into English it is "*kyooryoku*". The first part of this two-character word represents the strength of three persons engaged in a joint effort. The second part simply means "strength". Thus a literal translation would be: the strength derived through the involvement of at least three persons in a common task.

Of even greater interest is the fact that the first *kanji* character includes a symbol very much like a cross. In Buss' words, "Herein lies the secret of meaningful, lasting cooperation. As we rally 'round the cross, as we join hands and hearts in obedience to His call, we are workers together with him. There is no greater challenge!"

6
FINANCING MISSIONS IN THE FUTURE
by Eldon J. Howard

INTRODUCTION

We have been talking about some dynamic concepts this week. "We are at the beginning of an exciting era in Missions". Things are different than they were a few years ago. The strategy is changing and with this, structure must change. As Peter Drucker - "The Dean of Management" has said in his book, "Management - Tasks, Responsibilities, Practices", "Structure follows strategy"

As we begin to talk about financing missions in the future we must recognize we are coming into a fast moving era. If we are going to come out whole and victorious we must recognize careful planning and good administration is a requirement.

One part of careful planning and good administration is the financial management we use from day to day. It is going to become increasingly mandatory to take finance in as part of the senior planning. This is going to demand senior professionally trained expertise on your staff.

The one thing we can count on is change. Change in the future, change in missions, change in financing. We must be ready to be flexible. We must keep our eye on definite, long-range goals, even if change is required in strategy we will want to keep on heading towards the same goal.

As we begin to review the world we are coming into during the coming period of 1977-1985 or until the Lord comes (whichever comes first) we note some complex problems facing mankind:

Eldon J. Howard, presently the International Comptroller for the Sudan Interior Mission, served in Nigeria, Ghana and Liberia before becoming the U.S. Treasurer of the S.I.M. He is doing graduate work at Rutgers toward an M.A. in Public Administration, is chairman of the Accounting Task Force of the IFMA and has recently completed a discussion draft of Standards of Accounting and Financial Reporting for Mission Organizations.

1. Poverty in the midst of plenty.
2. Degradation of our environment.
3. Loss of faith in our institutions.
4. Insecurity of employment.
5. Rejection of traditional values.
6. Economic and other monetary and economic disruptions.

However, we have always found man is very creative in developing alternative methods to handle problems.

These problems occur in all societies. The reason they appear as problems which defy analysis, is that they interact. We try to look at each one specifically, but when we do, we forget the others.

We forget the trends, origins, significance and interrelationship of the various components and thus are unable to devise effective responses or plans. We find it most difficult to work within very complex, large, intricate systems.

Exhibit A tells you where we are going this morning.

Exhibit A

Financing Missions in the Future
Outline

1. A Priori Assumptions

2. Developing World Trends

    - Phases of growth
    - Technological developments
    - Government trends

3. Mission Trends

    - Program activities
    - Supporting services activities

4. Planning the Financing

A PRIORI ASSUMPTIONS

Let us begin with two points of reference we will use as our a priori assumptions.

1. Jesus is coming soon.
2. Our study of God's Word shows that when Jesus came last time, all world conditions had been coordinated perfectly for maximization of outreach of the gospel. God is going to do it again before Christ's second coming. We have only to tie into His plan.

             We can expect – financial
                          – linguistical
                          – political
                          – sociological
                          – cultural
                          – legal
                          – strategical

All phases of the world will be in perfect coordination so that every nation will have had the chance to make a decision for or against Jesus Christ.

DEVELOPING WORLD TRENDS

In reviewing world trends, lets look at these through the set of filters of planners and financial managers in our mission setting.

First lets look at the worlds in which we live and work.

- Each one of our missons is different because of the different locations and cultures we work with.

- Each one of the countries we work in is at a different stage of development.

Therefore, as a basis for looking at world trends we have to set up a basis that will be meaningful to each of us. I would like to develop a model which has 3 parts:

- Pre-Industrial Era
- Industrial Era
- The Post Industrial Era

I believe the context will help us define these terms. I am using this type of model so that you can mentally picture your countries, or segments of some countries or situations you know.

This will also help you look at each one in the same way we look at our children. Each one is special, each one is different, each one is at a different place in their development.

Exhibit B

Phases of Growth
Economic

Pre-Industrial	Industrial	Post-Industrial

- Extractive Industry
  -farm
  -fish
  -mining
  -forestry
	- Service Industry
	  -marketing
	  -manufacturing
	  -construction
	  -transportation
	  -finance
	    -bank
	    -insurance
	  -government
	    -defense
		- Life Style
		  -health, edu-
		   cation, wel-
		   fare, of sick
		   & old
		
		- Arts
		  -music, sculp-
		   ture, drama,
		   cooking
		
		- Leisure acti-
		  vities
		  -travel
		  -non-voca-
		   tional skills

Every economy basically goes through three phases of econ-omic growth.

1. Pre-Industrial

During this period primary activities are extractive, prin-cipally agriculture, mining, forestry, fishing. The society therefore spends most of its time contending with nature. Nor-mally, there is a much higher proportion of people in the rural areas than in the urban areas. This is typical of the majority of areas that we have been working in during the past decade.

2. Industrial

As a society advances, the areas of marketing, manufacturing, and construction grow. The society then begins to contend with both nature and materials. This era begins as a service econ-omy for the primary activities, this latter develops to pro-vide other service industry with activities including banking, transportation, insurance, and government. During the indus-trial era, offensive and defensive warfare takes on added im-portance.

As technology develops, nature and materials take on less and less significance; affluence increases. This leads to a society and culture moving from the suburban to the urban life style. As this continues, the struggle moves away from contention with nature and materials and moves toward contention with organizations, power and prestige. This is where the remainder of our missionary tasks are, and where our home churches are, today.

3. Post-Industrial

Eventually as technology and industrialization conquer the extractive, construction and service eras, a new type of culture develops. Human endeavor will spend less and less of its time in the primary and secondary tasks and will perform more tasks for the tasks' sake. Ends become less important. Means increase in importance. This is the era we in the U.S. and Canada are just coming into. Activities which we now regard as leisure time activities will increase in importance. These would include - reading, writing, art, music, done for their own sake; gourmet cooking, an aristocratic formal life style, or hunting, fishing, camping, hiking, boating, for fun not livelihood. Acquisition of non-vocational skills, travel to explore new places, cultures, and ideas.

During this type of era, social security, welfare, health care, public works, and improving the general life style become more important.

Because of the lack of a challenge for survival, man becomes more and more involved with "inner space exploration" so the evoking of images of splendor, pride, pomp, awe, communal, ethnic, religious, or national unity or identity take on greater meaning and importance.

For some during this era - the non-productive pressures will be too much and they will "cop out" instead of trying to help define the objectives. We have recently seen a great deal of this begin to happen over the past 10 years. This transition is difficult.

The era we are entering is probably the most difficult. We are now going into an era where there are no guideposts to define achievement. Survival, of course. Earning a living, very easy - but what do I do of value? What has meaning?

Economic growth in the post-industrial era poses some very interesting - highly motivational challenges and dynamic opportunities for the church, such as we have never before seen - if we will capture them.

Exhibit C

Phases of Growth
Social

Pre-Industrial	Industrial	Post-Industrial
-Social		
-Self Reliant	-Cooperative	-Free Form
-rigid	-flexible	-less self dis-
-individualistic	-organized	cipline
-thoughtful	-participation	-institutional
-survival	-belonging	-selfish
		-rights
-Personal		
-External Exploration	-Technological	-Internal
-land	development	exploration
-sea		
-air	-Organization	-inner self
	development	-religious
		-nationalistic

Society is changing from being self reliant and individualistic to becoming institutionalized and rights demanding.

Personal motivation will change from survival against nature to survival within the system - with a few wanting to manage the system.

Men and women <u>knew</u> they were accomplishing something of value <u>when</u> they could survive against nature and bring up a family to help them survive in the future. They belonged, they had won, they had a reason for life.

As a society moves into the post-industrial era survival is no longer a question. Basic needs are no longer a problem. Why raise a family? What is worth striving for? What is really of importance? What can I give myself to that is of value?

This is the world we are moving into. People are going to need to belong to something! They are going to want to be part of something of value! Something eternal.

The United Nations in September 1975 introduced "The New International Economic Order" - The name tag for the new

economic system toward more equitable sharing of world resources.
This plan suggests that the rich minority of the world begin to
help the poor majority to develop their countries. Economic
training and aid will begin to help the majority of countries to
not only begin to complete their pre-industrial era but move
successfully into the industrial era. This will accomplish two
things:

1. Help the standard of living:
2. Correct the potential over population question.
    We are going to see increased pressure in these
    areas and lots of money to help it happen.

Gross world production (the GNP - for the world) will see
dynamic increases over the next few years. The rich will get
richer. The poor will get percentage wise much richer.

Current per capita income in the U.S. and Canada is about
$7,000 per annum. This will increase by 40% in real terms over
the next 8 years.

By comparison in the less developed countries the average
$150 to $200 will probably increase by 100-150% to around $400
to $500 during the same period.

What does this mean to us - missions. Two things:

1. The local congregations will have increasing amounts of
money to sponsor the programs of developing the local church
themselves.

2. For development of their congregations in agriculture
and self development economic projects, we can get all the
money we can intelligently use. This can cause very serious
problems.

God can keep missions poor for one reason - we haven't been
able to handle money intelligently. In fact, we haven't even
felt it was important.

How many missions have treasurers who are on your senior
decision-making councils as full time voting members - very few.
The objectives of missions are not financial, so finance has
never been important, so God has not supplied the finances. If
we mean business for God, we need the money to do the job. This
means we have to start by recognizing finance as an integral
part of the planning activity. "It's the foolish man who starts
a building without first counting the cost," Jesus is recorded
to have said to the old financier named Matthew.

Exhibit D

Phases of Growth
Technological Developments

Pre-Industrial	Industrial	Post-Industrial
-Population		
-High birth rate for survival	-Medium birth rate for maintenance	-Low birth rate for future
-Food		
-Famine	-Maintenance	-Excess
-Fuel		
-Extractive	-Extractive	-Harness available
-Difficult	-Development	-Excess
-Raw Materials		
-Visable	-Locatable	-Imaginative alternatives

Population Developments

For the next 5-6 years we will continue to see, in the current under-developed countries, high population growth rates continue. The possibility of famine, disease, short life span, need for help when parents are old, will require people to feel this need. However, as the economic/agricultural programs are developed - this growth rate will begin to turn down. This is what has happened in the developed countries, who are going from the industrial to the post-industrial phases of growth.

Food, Fuel, Raw Materials

As you can see on Exhibit D as we move from the pre-industrial to the industrial phases, technological development helps to increase the food, fuel, and raw materials available. Existence of these is not the problem. We, the people - and our understanding of how to use these resources, - is the only problem.

Exhibit E

Phases of Growth
World Trends

Pre-Industrial	Industrial	Post-Industrial
-Governments		
-Local government control	-Federal government control (Nationalistic)	-World government control

- Tax
- Law and order
	- Tax
	- Law and order
	- Education
	- Welfare
	  -aged
	  -sick
	   *survival life
	   style
	-Development
	  -agriculture
	  -industry
	  -resources
		- Tax
		- Law and order
		- Education
		- Welfare
		  -aged
		  -sick
		   *minimum life
		   style
		-Development
		  -agriculture
		  -industry
		  -resources
		  -population
		-Protection
		  -rights
		  -fraud

Methods of Financing Government

- Extractive	- Cooperative	- Inflation

World Trends

Exhibit E shows the trends that are apparent in the style
of government, the methods of financing the increase of government involvement and the methods established for paying for
government and other goods and services.

Exhibit F

Phases of Growth
World Trends

Pre-Industrial	Industrial	Post-Industrial
Methods of Trade		
– Barter	– Banking – Foreign exchange	– Controlled – One world currency – World economic order
– Goods and services	– Money	– Automatic transfer between bank accounts

Just a few more things as we look into the trends we see coming in the next few years as they affect our world.

1. Futurology will take on a much greater importance. The present and its relation to the future will be of interest. The past will become of less and less interest.

2. Mode of money transfer will become more mechanized and standardized throughout the world. A world currency will be increasingly accepted and utilized.

3. Corporations will become more socially conscious and will increasingly make funds and personnel available.

4. Personal discretionary funds will increase both at home and abroad. So both the local church there and here will have more real money than they have ever had before. They will increasingly use it for things they feel are of value. They will have to be convinced that missions – the mission of the church – is of value. But once convinced, money will not be a problem.

MISSION TRENDS

With that view as to where the world around us is going, now lets turn to how all of this scenario is going to affect us in missions.

First, we are going to increasingly have to clearly define, as an organization, what our mission's objectives are, why we want to do it, how we are going to accomplish those objectives, what financial and personnel resources we will need, when we will accomplish these obejctives, and how we will know that they have completed them.

Exhibit G

Planning Wheel

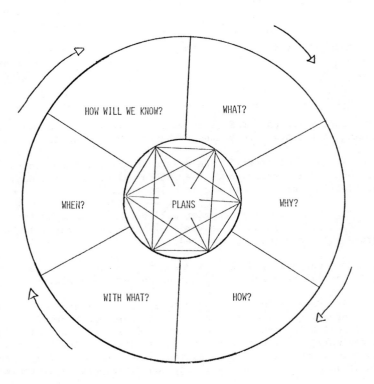

A good plan of action <u>must</u> come down to a <u>monetary</u> <u>and</u> numerical plan defining what are the realistic goals or objectives of the organization for the coming year. (and years)

A good plan must include a budget. Budgets are good. We all agree. But the art of preparing and using a budget is completely foreign to most missionary organizations. It's not that the director, treasurer, or board is unaware of their importance, more that we lack the desire and possibly the skill to apply budgeting techniques to a missionary organization. We unconsciously argue - our goals are not financial, so budgets really are not applicable to us.

This type of thinking will put a mission out of existence in the world that is coming. Missions and our members have traditionally avoided being managed by anyone. As the world changes this may be a luxury we may not be able to continue to retain. Between the government and the economies - good sound financial planning and coordinating principles will become a requirement.

1. This is going to cost money!
2. This will require organizational discipline!
3. This is going to require a financial member on our organization's senior management team. A voting member on our senior policy body <u>who is trained</u> in financial management.

This type of person will pay for himself many times over, just in cash flow management. This is something a good bookkeeper knows almost nothing about.

We have talked about the world trends we see coming, but what is going to happen to missions? Missionary organizations are established for two basic reasons:

1. To bring people to Christ.
2. To teach them the Word of God so they can bring others to Christ.

In our effort to accomplish these tasks, we find we have to engage in eight types of program activities. The program activities outline the parts of our ministry that we are in a country to perform. These include those listed on Exhibit H. Let's use this as our outline for the next few minutes, to talk about financing missions.

Exhibit H

Mission Activities

A. Program Activities

    1. Bible schools and seminaries
    2. Church Growth and evangelism
    3. Education
    4. Linguistics
    5. Media
    6. Medical
    7. Relief and rehabilitation and community development
    8. Services to missionaries/churches

B. Supporting Service Activities

    1. Administration
    2. Fund raising
    3. Furlough ministry activities

1. Bible Schools, Seminaries and Scholarships

We all recognize that this is one of the most important parts of our ministry. We also recognize it is one of the
most difficult to raise money for because there are so many
competitors.

2. Church Growth and Evangelism

The front line - "real missionaries" are included here.
Out where the action is. This phase of our ministry has always
been able to attract all the money from the believers the
missions have felt was necessary. Often the only reason we
have not had more, was because we haven't asked.

I wonder why we have looked so little at the universities in our home countries as a way to evangelize those overseas? International Students are the only ones I know who are
doing very much with this.

Before we go any further, let's look at #1 and 2. Is
there any reason that the ongoing operating expenses of Bible
schools, seminaries and the church cannot be completely financed by the local congregations with the exception of possibly
the missionary and the capital developments?

Expect that the economic growth in the countries we are ministering in are going to grow so that this will become a reality in a very short time except for a brand new pioneer work.

3. Education

As each country comes into the industrial era, the local governments begin taking over the schools.

The impact of this is that:

a. They will finance the education system, - if not all at least part.

b. They will define the curriculum, however, they will be open for consultants to help. Especially if the consultants are knowledgeable in both the field of education and their country. What an ideal way to influence a country for Christ and in some cases on the government's payroll.

c. They will begin to manage the systems, let them have the administrative headaches.

d. They will, in some cases, be thankful if missionary organizations can locate good teachers for them to hire. This again gives open doors for Christ.

Expect the need for financing of education programs to diminish rapidly, over the next 8-10 years.

4. Translation and Linguistics

a. This will never be totally financed locally.

b. Expect that translation will go faster as trained bilinguals begin to do the translation work.

c. Take a close look at the possibility of translation and linguistic work being done outside of closed countries, possibly combining further Bible study in work/study programs for the brightest students. Then short trips for consultation and workshops.

d. Linguists are going to be less and less welcome in foreign countries so we must begin to develop imaginative alternatives.

5. Media

    a. Expensive

    b. Wide distribution

    c. In order to maximize effectiveness, it must be part of a total coordinated effort! This requires extra planning but the planning can provide results all out of proportion to the time and effort.

    d. <u>Increased</u> local financing but the majority will come from home.

    e. Of all the program activities, this one demands the most business hardheadness or you are pouring money down a never ending hole.

6. Medical

    a. In many countries the day of missions institutional medicine is finished.

    b. Two ways we can be involved are:

        1). Working under the government sponsored programs (sure helps the financing).
        2). Working in community health projects for which there are large amounts of both local and foreign government subsidy funds available.

Foundations and organizations have been developed the past few years to support a great deal of this type of work.

    c. For countries where hospitals aren't yet being taken over, ask why? During the next few years, at least, the financing will be or should be taken over and in light of this, ask very real questions about putting any mission funds into medical institutions. Foundation and government funds are available if needed.

    d. As local personnel begin taking over clinics they will find here is a real profit to be made. We must be sure we have trained sound Christian business men who know how to use the funds in the Lord's economy.

7. <u>Relief, Rehabilitation and Community Development</u>

Lack of money has nothing to do with this question. There is more money than you can intelligently use. The biggest financial problem here is how to not let it swallow you up, so that you lose sight of the objectives. You can so ruin a local economy that people will take your food and good works and then spit on you, not glorify your Father which is in heaven. You can split your mission and frustrate your personnel beyond measure with too much money for relief work.

Governments are beginning to realize aid has been counter-productive. Anything but the teaching and training at the grass roots level is going to be phased out in the R & R area. Meeting short term emergencies must be done with greatest care and planning.

Don't let the easy money define your objectives. Some of the most well-meaning people, can lead you off course as to why you are on location.

8. Services to Missionaries

    a. Increasingly these are available locally or can be supplied by local personnels.

    b. They are expensive!

    c. Missionaries are demanding better care. They are more conscious of the value of their time.

        - travel,
        - communications,
        - housing,
        - health care needs.

All very important, but review regularly the need for mission personnel to perform these services during the next few years.

    d. This is something which must be financed from within the mission.

Lets summarize the programs

    1. More money will be available locally. We should expect local partnership.

    2. More money is available for meeting physical and intellectual needs. We can expect to find all we can use.

    3. Money must be provided for meeting the media, translation, and training of the church for tommorrow from the saints at home. It will be available if we plan and communicate our plans.

Supporting Service Activities

1. Administration

Because of the various government requirements we are
going to have to spend more time administering and reporting.
We must be very careful that we don't just establish
"make work" programs for everyone who can't return to their
field of work. We demand a professional in an operating room
of a hospital, <u>demand</u> the same level of expertise in the accounting, shipping, purchasing, and personnel management areas, <u>and</u>
then be willing to <u>listen</u> to them.

A financial professional can cut costs a lot more than
hiring cheap help - even if they are ex-missionaries.

We have to recognize there are some very real costs
coming as the large flux of missionaries who went out in the
1930's and 1940's begin to retire. Watch very carefully as the
laws develop in this area. Missions have not, by and large prepared sufficiently for the retirement of their missionaries.

Let me share something with you. During the next few
years the <u>churches and friends are going to stop supporting</u> any
and all of our retired missionaries. We can't count on money
from them in our planning. Ten years from now we won't be
getting it. They expect that we are getting it from them now -
while our missionary is active.

It's an administrative responsibility to have made the
provision for these folk. We can count on more generosity in
the States for these folk, as we now have in Canada. Some
questions will have to be answered:

> - Are we ready to admit we haven't properly provided
>   for our missionaries so that they can obtain the
>   extra subsidies the government will give the poor? -
>   - or -
> - Are we ready to put a greater portion into our re-
>   tirement programs now to prepare for this?

<u>Financing</u> the administration should be part of the cost
of an ongoing program. Into every program cost should be a
portion for administration. The Canadian government expects a
10% administration charge to cover home office expenses. They
expect the field supervision and management expenses will be
covered out of the remaining 90%.

This should also be true of any thinking donor.

We have some who haven't really considered the problem.
We must educate them.

Administration costs are going to be more expensive.
But let me give a ray of hope - <u>inflation</u> is going to help us.
Yes, inflation. If we keep the support requirement up-to-date
with the foreign Cost of Living changes in order to keep our
missionaries whole, because costs are growing more rapidly away
from North America, you will have a proportionately greater
amount of money to work with-to give the administrative support
to the field team.

Wise financial planning by our organization can make
major differences in being able to cover administrative costs
both at home and on the field.

Look for men of years and experience who can retire at
50-55, (set a second retirement date of 65 so you don't find
yourself in trouble) or look for younger men who God is calling
into this field. There are a lot of them around. Note of
caution - if you get them - listen or you will lose them.

2. <u>Fund Raising</u>

Fund raising costs are becoming more and more expensive.
Just mail costs bear this out. We should see a proportionate
larger amount of funds available because of the growth of <u>dis-
cretionary funds</u> available to the folk at home.

A major challenge missions must accept is to teach
pastors and congregations how to live in a day of affluence.
God is now supplying the money and He will be doing so in abundance. You look at the average church's parking lot on Sunday
morning and count the cars over 5 years old! Christians have
money! They want to do something significant! They want to
know how! We must help them see the validity of a Christian's
life style.

<u>Corporations</u> also are becoming more social responsibili-
ty conscious, expect and see increased funds and personnel from
corporations, leave of absence personnel can be a big help.

Nothing has been more important in fund raising than the
<u>real live missionary</u>. Be careful about short furloughs. It
supplies the golden egg, but can kill the goose.

The old mission representatives, with the same old stories about 30 years ago in the jungle has got to change. Missionaries and reps must have the sales tools, know what they are

going to say, and how to say it, with positive enthusiasm!!
We - missions - have to help wake up the church at home who are
getting restless. They have the money, have the time and want
to be involved. (In spite of the hurry around us)

Foundations and governments will require a knowledgeable
senior person coordinating all approaches to them from our organization. An ideal position for a good senior executive.

So, again let's summarize.

1. Administration is expensive and necessary.
2. Administration is a legitimate part of the program
and as such deserves a reasonable part of the supporting
funds.
3. Wise administration by knowledgeable administrators
will bring in dollars through wise cash management and
reduced expenses.
4. Money will be increasingly available for responsible
organizations. Christians at home want to be involved
if the program is valid and they can get their companies
involved.
5. Missionaries properly trained and with good tools
are our best fund raisers.
6. Dealing with foundations and governments should be
coordinated by senior executives of our organization.
7. Deferred giving - very important - we will talk
about that a bit later.

PLANNING THE FINANCING

Financial strength depends on the desire of the organization to be strong and to be accountable.

Accountability

A growing demand by governments and society to tell them
our plans - remember our earlier planning wheel? What, why,
how, with what, when and how will we know.

This type of planning must be developed into every part of
our organization! Mind you it will shake some folk, but then
change to a more productive system always does.

Planning like this demands honest accountability to:

1. The Lord
2. Myself
3. My colleagues

4. My board
5. My staff
6. My donors

That's hard.

Accountability like this requires a new type of reporting which will soon be demanded by all governments instead of
only some. A type of reporting that says more than just - "The
money came and now it's gone." This "it's gone" type of reporting
has been followed for years by missionary organizations. It has
really hurt us. It hasn't helped us plan, be accountable, train
those working with us at home or abroad, or helped us really
know where we've been, where we are or where we're going.

To assist in developing the type of reporting we, as
missions, need so badly - a year ago, the IFMA and EFMA established an IFMA-EFMA Accounting Task Force working under the IFMA
Business Administration Committee.

It has developed a guide to assist us in meeting the demands which we increasingly face. Governments and foundations
want to see accounting methods which clearly reflect our financial activities. We have a story we can be proud of. Our
effectiveness with the use of funds has been proven. We must
now provide a system to demonstrate it to the public.

We have talked fast. We have covered a lot of ground in
the past hour. We have talked about why finance will be available, what we can anticipate in world trends, the program trends
and supporting trends and the need to manage our financing and
financial reporting. I'm thankful that we know:

1. Jesus is coming soon.
2. He is preparing the world, the economies, the social
systems, the populations, the governments, the resources,
His people, for His coming! I'm thankful to be a part!
Aren't you?

A discussion draft of <u>Standards of Accounting and Financial Reporting for Mission Organizations</u> is available by sending $3.50
to the IFMA Accounting Task Force, Box C, Cedar Grove, N.J. 07009.

7

FOUR BIG CHALLENGES MISSIONS WILL FACE IN THE NEXT DECADE

by Richard Oestreicher

The future will bring changes. How can we cope with the problems of the next decade and take advantage of the opportunities that are already in the making?

In this session, we will be outlining some of the areas that will demand our time and efforts, identifying some of the arenas where we will be wrestling in the next five to ten years.

This is not to scare, or to say "what's the use?", but to forewarn, to prepare, and to begin to seek solutions early.

1. THE CHALLENGE OF INCOMPLETE MANAGEMENT

One Christian fundraising counsellor said, "I shudder to think what would happen if some of the organizations I help actually got the money they were looking for. They think they have financial problems. What they really have are management problems. Being poor has kept them out of trouble.

A. The Fundamental Objectives

What are we to accomplish - in terms that are specific and measurable?

How else can we know where we are strong and weak, whether trends are working for us or against us, or if we are nearing conclusion?

Richard Oestreicher is presently Director of Donor Relations of the Far Eastern Gospel Crusade. After service in the army in the Far East, he first served as Treasurer and later Business Manager of the F.E.G.C. He holds the M.B.A. degree in Business Administration from the University of Michigan and is a member of the Business Administration Committee of the IFMA.

B. Long Range Planning

Traditionally we are responders, next-step people,
rather than long range planners.

Plans we've made are more like dreams, because we've
not developed control mechanisms.

We need to work on developing information channels for
input rather than relying on subjective assumptions.

We'll need a strong inner commitment to planning. It is
hard, takes time and is easily replaced by temporarily
urgent matters.

Various alternate plans must be worked out to cover
changes in personnel, funds, and political situations.

C. Management of Personnel

Missions will need to actually supervise and lead their
personnel and move away from the laissez-faire approach
to personnel administration.

Personnel departments will no longer fulfill their
task by merely recruiting, orientating and delivering
new missionaries to ministry locations. Personnel
management will include a continuous process of growth
and development.

D. What's Happening Now?

We are reading, studying and discussing management,
planning and personnel concepts like never before.

We are growing in our ability to receive and apply
advice from outside our own IFMA/EFMA spheres.

2. THE CHALLENGE OF RISING PUBLIC DEMANDS AND GOVERNMENTAL
REGULATION

One attorney feels this will be our biggest headache. He
predicts the day will soon come when each mission will need
a full time attorney on its staff.

A. Consumerism

Demands for disclosure of financial information will
increase. Some of us will have to "admit" we really do
have fundraising costs.

Responding to questionnaires from supporting churches
has risen to problematical dimensions. ACMC pledges to
work with EFMA/IFMA to devise an approach to providing
churches with necessary information.

Mailing practices will be questioned as an invasion of
privacy.

If missions are reluctant to disclose information,
expose practices, or cooperate whole-heartedly, we will
see the rise of an organized Christian public.

B. Governmental Interference

Piece-meal taxation on the local level in the form of
charges for certain public services.

States, interested in protecting the populace, will
look more carefully into our financial practices and
policies. Contracts, loan arrangements, gift annuities
and other areas of planned giving will become regulated.

Pension plans, financial reporting (reporting income by
named donors), continued tax-exemption of some functions,
and discrimination will be new issues as we relate to
the U.S. Treasury Department.

C. What's Happening Now?

Most missions are open as never before to outside scru-
tiny. We're looking at mission accounting and reporting
to provide public information. As we adopt it, we'll
benefit even more from the new management information
it provides us.

3. THE CHALLENGE OF INCREASED ECONOMIC PRESSURES

Economic problems are predicted most frequently by friends
of missions as a serious future difficulty.

A. Runaway International Inflation

Missionary support cost will continue to rise, perhaps
out of proportion to salaries and wages of North
American contributors.

Foreign currency exchange rates will fluctuate with
increasing frequency.

IFMA/EFMA may consider the possibility some day of an inter-mission international payment clearing house to maximize benefits from exchange rate fluctuations.

B. Administrative Costs

Pressures will come within our mission for more and better publications, recruiting and other services.

Reporting to our public and to governmental units will add substantially to our costs.

C. Donor's Own Pressures

Inflation is here to stay. Unemployment among our constituents will probably never go away. Housing costs are soaring, especially for newly established homes. It will be increasingly difficult for us to attract numbers of young adults into our supporting constituency.

We must regularly interpret the constant changes in the way income comes to us and discover what messages are there for us.

D. Slow Growth in Income

The Christian world in North America is not rapidly expanding, not as fast as our financial needs are expanding.

Unless we take deliberate steps in some new directions, we will see intensified competition in funding our works. Some communities have a banquet almost every other week.

Planned giving can be helpful as an income source, but must be soundly and wisely administered, or it can bury us. And when one Christian organization fails, we all suffer.

E. What's Happening Now?

Financial pressures are forcing organizations to budget and plan financially. We are learning the skills we'll need to cope with the pressures.

Well-managed computer assistance in performing some functions is growing among us.

We are cooperating as never before in mission ministries "over there", and in problem solving "here at home". When cooperation characterizes some of our approaches to funding, we will have taken a big step forward.

More and more we are engaged in honest self-analysis. We are growing in our ability to see both our strengths and our weaknesses.

Inflation in North America has helped our donors to understand what our missionaries have been trying to say for several years. And they are responding with real care and concern.

4. THE CHALLENGE OF INTERACTING WITH THE NORTH AMERICAN CHRISTIAN'S WORLD VIEW.

    A. Ultimate Value of Missionary Activity

        People will always ask, "Why keep sending missionaries overseas?" After events such as Cambodia and Viet Nam, they are heard more frequently.

    B. Foreign Involvement

        Some people will become more "World" conscious; others will become isolationistic as the world political situation grows more complex.

        The rise of foreign economies, and their impact upon our own economy, will make some people reluctant to invest in ministries to the developed nations.

    C. Mission or National

        Supporting national Christian workers overseas is a hot idea now. We must work to see this become all it should be, with proper relationships in all directions.

        It's wrong that it is easier to find full funding for a missionary to crank a printing press in Africa than to find support for an African, even though his cost may be only half that of the North American missionary.

    D. Fads, Fancies, and Frustrations

        Disaster relief, hunger, orphans, seem to dominate the Christian press as missions. That is a real part, but

only a part of the picture. We must communicate the
totality and the fundamental objectives of our organizations.

In theory, donors have some difficulties with the
pressures that a personalized support method places
on the missionary, but in giving practice, donors like
the method. If theory eventually modifies practice,
some of our organizations will need to adapt accordingly.

E. What's Happening Now?

ACMC is on the scene. Its concern and helpfulness will
assist both the supporting church and mission agencies
to better understanding and relationships.

Contributors are traveling to missionary locations more
than ever before. This has to help proper understanding
and better world view.

Mission and missionary communications are more honest,
genuine and human than they have ever been.

Two Scripture verses apply that will serve to encourage us.
The first is a favorite paraphrase of Romans 8:28. "Everything
makes sense -- ultimately!"

The second comes from II Corinthians 8:12. "For the
service the ministering of this fund renders, not only meets the
needs of all the saints (the overseas believers and the missionaries), but also results in many cries of thanksgiving to God
(not only from those benefited, but from the donors as well).

If we're doing our job as mission administrators well, this
is going to happen.

8

EDUCATION TODAY FOR MISSION TOMORROW

by *Edwin L. Frizen, Jr.*

Church mission relations is increasingly becoming an important area of dialogue between mission agencies and the sending or supporting churches in North America. This is resulting in creative innovation and involvement in mission on the part of local church mission committees, pastoral staff, and church members.

The focus of this presentation is education in the local church. Since the mission board is actually the sending arm of the church, education for mission demands the involvement and combined, cooperative efforts of the church and the mission agency.

MISSION INVOLVEMENT

For maximum effectiveness in the future program of world evangelization, the mission agency must be adequately staffed at home and overseas, as well as adequately supported financially. Both the staff and the finances come from the local church. Therefore, the mission must be actively and responsibly involved in education for mission in the local church.

Denominational mission boards will coordinate their involvement with their denomination's Christian education department or division. Interdenominational or independent mission agencies, which have a large number of supporting independent local churches, have a greater responsibility to provide helps for year-around mission education.

Edwin L. (Jack) Frizen, presently Executive Director of the Interdenominational Foreign Mission Association, after serving in the army during World War II returned to help found the Far Eastern Gospel Crusade, working for four years as Home Secretary and Treasurer. For the following eight years he was Business Manager and Treasurer of the FEGC in the Philippines. For the last thirteen years he has headed up the office of the IFMA. He holds the M.A. degree from Wheaton College and an M.S. from Florida State University.

Response to a follow up questionnaire on the effects of Green Lake '71 by IFMA missions demonstrated that some missions have taken quite seriously their responsibility to improve relationships with constituent churches. The primary action indicated was an increase in the representative of pastors added to mission councils, boards and committees.

There was indication that missions were increasing their regional representatives who have primary responsibility to work with local churches, offering various helps in the area of mission education. These regional representatives help coordinate the furlough deputation of missionaries throughout their area. Several missions indicated that they have increased their mission education presentations at pastors' conferences and other local and inter-church meetings.

In checking the titles of IFMA mission executives, it is surprising to note only the Latin America Mission has a Director of Church Ministries. The Overseas Christian Servicemen's Centers has a Director of Public Ministries. Arctic Missions sponsors two and three-day schools of mission seminars for local congregations and one-day pastors' seminars, and received help in the area of church mission relations by the 1966 Wheaton Congress and GL '71.

Mission education in North America now includes a major emphasis on the overseas church. Overseas church leaders are increasingly invited to North America to share their vision and burden for the Lord's work in their countries and continents.

Missions have increased their help to local church mission education through brochures and how-to-do-it articles in mission periodicals. Some missions publish detailed annual reports with graphs and statistics which can be used by supporting churches in their mission education programs.

MISSION EDUCATION IN THE LOCAL CHURCH

In the past, some churches seemingly gave very little thought to a planned program of missionary education for their various departments and activities. For some, the missionary emphasis was left to articles in Christian magazines, church publications and some reference to missions in Sunday School materials. In other cases, the occasional visit of a missionary, or possibly even a missionary conference, was expected to give the congregation the needed missionary emphasis. At best, such measures were able to provide only limited information without relationship to an overall plan of churchwide mission education.

THE PASTOR

For an effective program of missionary education, the pastor and other leaders of the church should be involved in promoting missionary concern among the members of the congregation. The vision of the pastor is one of the most important factors in the success of any missionary education program. The pastor sets the priorities for the different emphases that are to be included in the total educational ministry of the church. The pastor should set the example and include missionary instruction in his preaching ministry.

However, the pastor alone cannot effectively handle the total program of missionary education. His staff of assistants-- paid or volunteer -- must relieve him of the routine details of the ongoing educational program of which missions education is a part.

THE MISSIONS COMMITTEE

The missions committee should keep a current inventory of personnel resources within the church family or community who can be called upon to assist in the church's program of mission education and outreach. Such resource personnel include mission staff, board members, leaders of Christian organizations and schools, missionary parents or other relatives, returned missionaries and short-term workers, missionary children and missionaries on furlough.

The missions committee should see that each of its members has some specific assignment for which he or she is responsible. Possible assignments include:

1. Responsibility for maintaining contact with and files on one or more mission agencies.

a. Share with missionaries and missions each year the church's missions committee membership, guidelines or mandate. Ask for suggestions or ideas in return.

b. Request from missionaries and missions a copy of their annual reports and other pertinent information.

2. Responsibility to review specific mission books and literature, sharing pertinent information with pastoral staff, missions committee, church librarian, Christian education workers and teachers.

a. Books, biographies, magazines and other literature received from mission organizations supported by the church.

b. General books on mission history and strategy.

c. Publications of inter-mission agencies such as IFMA News, Evangelical Missions Quarterly, Missionary News Service, EMIS Pulse editions, etc. Information provided in these publications will help to strengthen the relationship between the local church and mission agencies.

3. Arrange for occasional consultation with a selected mission leader.

4. Arrange for visits to North American headquarters of selected missions.

5. Encourage field visits, short-term missionary assignments, as well as career missionary service by members of the congregation.

6. Encourage church members to consider service on the home staff of a mission agency. Secretarial help is one of the most consistent needs of mission offices.

7. Work to develop a dynamic relationship with a few selected mission boards rather than trying to maintain an equal relationship with a long list of missions.

a. Start with one mission agency to which the church is already contributing through the support of the ministry of one or more of its missionaries.

b. Study available books, periodicals and leaflets relating to this mission.

c. Arrange for personal contact with representatives of the mission including use of missionaries to teach in the mission education program of the church when available.

d. Consider together mutual goals of world evangelization shared by the church and mission.

EDUCATION IN MISSION FINANCE

The day of inexpensive missions is over. In many cases, the total missionary salary is now comparable to the salary of a pastor or member of the pastoral staff. Churches should endeavor to support the ministry of workers sent out from the

church as they do resident staff workers. In other words, consider the missionary as associate pastor or a Christian education
director. This means that the local church should assume the
major financial responsibility for missionaries from its own
congregation.

The local church should:

1. Maintain a current inventory of the financial needs of
each missionary project within the interest of the church.

2. Determine financial share which the church will undertake to raise for a mission toward the ministry of a member of
the congregation who enters missionary service. This policy
should be shared frequently with the congregation.

3. Determine the share the church will undertake to raise
for other mission ministries.

4. Consider additional regular contributions to the general
fund of any mission supported by the church. Designated contributions can also be made toward the ministry of North American
headquarters staff.

COORDINATOR OF EDUCATION IN MISSION

A chairman or coordinator of missionary education has been
utilized with good results in some churches. This person or
committee must relate well with the pastor and pastoral staff,
including the director of Christian education, chairman of the
Christian Education Committee, superintendent of the Sunday
school, and any other educational leaders within the church
program. One of the major responsibilities of the missions
education coordinator or chairman is to work with the other
church education leaders for an overall plan for integrating
missions education into the planned curriculum and program of
every department and activity of the church.

Christian young people do respond on occasion to the
prompting of the Holy Spirit and make a commitment for possible
missionary service after a missionary message. However, too
often such decisions are not followed with any special program
of missionary education in the local church. Such training is
often delayed until a young person enrolls in Bible college.
This, of course, often limits missionary training to the few who
persist in their desire to follow the call of the Lord at all
costs. Tragically, there are many others who become sidetracked
because they really do not know how to follow through with the
decision which was made.

Any young person making a commitment indicating a desire
to serve the Lord in some missionary service should receive
special instruction under the supervision of the pastor and the
missions education committee coordinator.   Such a program would
result in many more young people formally preparing for missionary service in Bible schools, colleges, and seminaries.   Another
advantage is that this training is accomplished within the framework of the local church, rather than as an independent activity
without significant relationship to the church.   Too often the
church is not involved until it is asked to help provide the
financial needs of the prospective missionary.

A missionary internship program in the local church, or at
least under local church supervision, is excellent preparation
for missionary service.

The local church must not abdicate its responsibilities for
missionary education.   Christian schools and evangelical mission
agencies have often provided missionary education which more
properly is the responsibility of the local church.   The local
church should be more centrally involved in the selection,
training, commissioning and sending of missionaries.

CONCLUSION

Education today for mission tomorrow.   What does that mean?

It means simply if we are to accomplish the job of evangelizing the world in this generation, education in mission must
be incorporated into every age level of the local church's
educational program.   The church must know what missions is all
about.   It must understand its own role in world evangelization
through the mission board, the sending arm of the church.

The mission board must recognize its role in the educational
program of the local church.   The mission agency may have to
initiate the steps to involvement.   There must be responsible
and creative planning, a willingness to cooperate with and serve
the local church.

The church and the mission must work diligently toward
common objectives, always keeping in mind our common commitment
of bringing to God through redemption by the blood of Jesus
Christ those "out of every kindred, and tongue, and people, and
nation".

Education today for mission tommorrow means hastening the
return of our Lord Jesus Christ.   Let us, therefore, be workers
together as heirs of the grace of God.

9

PERSONNEL FOR TOMORROW'S MISSION

by Wilfred A. Bellamy

The subject is <u>Personnel for Tomorrow's Mission</u> . As I
have sat through the sessions revelling in the richness of the
fellowship, I have enjoyed the input which I personally feel is
perhaps the deepest and most heart searching that I have yet
experienced in the fellowship of EFMA/IFMA since the Lord first
gave me experience of that in 1969. I am glad for the title of
the session. It has about it an element of hope. It reminds
us that mission does have a future, and it is in the hands of
the people of God. The title also pre-supposes that God will
go on using people. I would love to think that God will go on
using me. I marvel that He does, but I love to think that it
is possible. I also love to think that I am looking at a group
of men and women this morning who are committed to be used of
God. There is a future for mission.

The title also raises the question, "What manner of people
and what manner of mission?" I want to use an illustration in
order to draw our thoughts to the substance of what I want to
share with you this morning. My thoughts will be wrapped up in
the word <u>relevance</u>.

Once upon a time there was a civilization where it was
thought by those who were elder that in order for a young man
to reach maturation and to be initiated into adult society, he
should master the art of spearing the spiney fish, be able to
club a woolly horse, and know how to hunt and catch a saber-
toothed tiger. If you have read the book "<u>The Saber-toothed
Curriculum</u>", that's what I'm speaking of. And so at a certain

---

Wilfred A. Bellamy, currently pastor of the Bloomfield Hills Baptist Church, worked under the Sudan United Mission in Nigeria.
He later directed the nationwide New Life for All Campaign in that
country before being called to Missionary Internship where he
served as Director until recently. He is a graduate of the University of London and has an M.A. in education from Michigan State
where he is now working on his doctorate.

time of his life, the young man would have to indulge in these
practices diligently until he had mastered them, because the
elders of the tribe deemed it important that he should. There
came a time, however, when by some strange freak of climatology,
the river dried up and no longer were there any spiney fish to
spear. As the water supply dried up, so did the trees cease to
flourish and the woolly horse had no where to hide, and was no
longer there to be clubbed. And the saber-toothed tiger that
preyed on the woolly horse no longer came down from the mountains,
and went to find other prey to feed upon. But there were criteria already established in that particular society that said
to be mature, a person must spear the spiney fish, and club the
woolly horse, and hunt the saber-toothed tiger and kill it.

What do you do when the elders have decided that certain
things are necessary, but they are no longer relevant. The
issue of relevance is a vital issue in the personnel for
tomorrow's mission. Not that they be relevant according to the
dictates of the elders, but that they be relevant according to
the needs of the people. So perhaps the emphasis will have to
change, and I do believe that under God, it is already changing,
away from the presuppositions of a home base mission agency to
a client orientation which asks first of all, "What is in the
best interests of those people in that place where we have been
given the responsibility for ministry?"

I am going to divide the remainder of the paper into two
parts. We will call them "Part A" and "Part B". The first
part gathers itself around the question, "What then can we say
about the people who are to be involved in a relevant mission
for tomorrow?" I am going to deal with this in three areas, and
there will be sub-sections to each area. The first area is in
the area of Biblical and Spiritual Absolutes. I have chosen
my words carefully, and I believe they are absolutely fundamental to mission. There are five Biblical and Spiritual
Absolutes, the first one is this: Unreserved Commitment to God.
If the people of tomorrow are to be relevant to the task, they
must first be committed to God. I put that first because I fear
that in our desire to see young men and women become missionaries
we tend to become task-oriented rather than God-oriented. We
see it in the manner in which we advertise -- we need two technicians, we need three doctors, we need four nurses, we need
six teachers, we need two church planters, and all of that.
And that is valid. But if our commitment is to select people
to fill slots, then we're missing the first premise -- the
vitality that is necessary in the life of the individual which
comes from a commitment to God and an awareness of God, and a
willingness to walk in holiness and righteousness with Him.
Being a missionary isn't having a job--it is being committed to
the person of God Himself.

Second, of the five absolutes - an <u>Awesome Sense of Respon-</u>
<u>sibility</u> of bearing the Gospel and its implication for every part
of life. We talk about evangelism, and we have used that slick
phrase "easy believism" and we despise it. We say any evangelism
that is easy believism is not evangelism. If the hearers have
not heard and understood the Gospel, they have not truly heard.
We use phrases of this type and believe them to be true, and yet
we bear about in our own lives a light-heartedness about the
service of our God. He has committed to His body to people like
you and me, an awesome responsibility to carry high upon our
hearts, a passion for men and women.

Third of the five absolutes is an <u>Awareness of a Need for</u>
<u>Resources</u> beyond himself. The missionary who feels he can cope
alone, probably cannot cope at all. There was a young man who
went down one day to the side of the river Jordan to cut wood,
and he was swinging away at the wood, and all of a sudden off
came the head of the axe into the water. He was at the end of
himself, and why, because he had lost his cutting edge. He
could have gone on swinging the haft of his axe against the tree
and making lots of noise ineffectually. But he was desperate.
He said, "Alas, master for it was borrowed." "I had resources
that were not of myself, and they have gone from me." The fundamental pre-requisite for all missionary Christian workers must
be an awareness of need for resources beyond himself.

Fourth of the five Biblical absolutes is a <u>Deep and Abiding</u>
<u>Dependency Upon God</u> which is manifested in a life of prayer. I
am old-fashioned enough to stand before you this morning, and
say I believe in a quiet time. A man who is marked by a life of
prayer, is a man who will be effective for God.

Fifth of the five absolutes is the <u>Holy Life which Models</u>
<u>the Message</u>. We have had a poignant reminder of this during
the week. I will not attempt to elaborate the point.

The second area in the first section of my paper deals with
<u>Essential Attitudes</u> that are based on these five Biblical abso-
lutes.

1. <u>A Sense of Being Securely Anchored in the Will of God</u>.
How would it be if one day, a missionary couple are driving
along and the wife says to the husband, "You got me into this."
That's a nice comforting feeling when you're in the heart of
Africa, isn't it? When a man or a woman of God has an attitude
which is born of the safety which comes to an individual who has
not only been called of God, but securely anchored in the Will of
God -- that is security! That is being where He wants you to be.

The missionary of tomorrow must understand that the Will of God is not something flippant and not something fickle -- that it's something solid and reliable and dependable as He is. Because it is in His very nature to have a sovereign will, and it's in the very nature of His people to stand in obedience to it.

2. A Healthy Sense of Self-Esteem. This does not imply a boastful, proud attitude, but a healthy awareness of your own person in God; an acceptance of self, shall we say.

3. A Secure Family Relationship, an attitude that is born of the ability to live in wholesomeness and harmony with those who are nearest and dearest to one. This will mean resolving past differences perhaps with parents, perhaps with one's more immediate loved ones. And a present wholesomeness within that relationship. Let me suggest this to you. From my ministry at Missionary Internship over the past five years, I have found that there is far less inner home security than you or I would care to believe among the young people of America today. This is one of the areas which is of critical significance. It is one of the areas that EFMA and IFMA have found sufficiently important to call a conference to talk about it in Farmington in December, 1976. If you can't reflect positively upon your ability to build at the home level an interpersonal relationship that sticks and works, then I suggest that the missionary going overseas is going to find it difficult to cope.

4. A Healthy Sense of Other-Person Esteem. A genuine respect for colleagues both missionary and national. Not judging them by Western criteria, and we have heard much about this. How absolutely vital it is that we recognize our oneness within the Body of Christ.

5. A Desire to Establish Close Relationships with Nationals. If your mission is purposed to train the national, may I honestly and humbly ask you, "Would you kindly take time to reflect upon the title or the purpose that you declare?" Here may well be the introduction into the thinking of the candidate to a phenomenon which may set him off on the wrong foot. At the very best you are a learner. Within the Body of Christ, we are all learners one of another and essentially of Him. Do you encourage missionaries to find his nurture in his national brother, and sit at the feet of the humble pastor who never went to the same kind of seminary, but has walked with God and knows what a holy life is all about. Here there might be mutual enrichment. Would you bear with me just two minutes as I share a word of personal testimony, not in any way to applaud my own missionary experience, but to share something that is real and touches me where I'm tender and I trust will say some-

thing to you. I had been a missionary in the Jarowa hills in
northern Nigeria for the better part of a year, and I knew just
how hopeless I was. You have never seen such an incompetent
missionary. I went to a Nigerian who was about 55 years of age
and who could barely read or write. I sat down with him, and I
said, "Would you be my Daddy?   Will you help me to be a missionary? Will you teach me how to live among your people, so that I
can be relevant to their needs?" When he saw that this was out
of a genuine attitude, he said, "I'll do it."

Some months later when my wife and I were separated by illness and I was alone, a knock came at the door. I hadn't been
home more than a couple of hours, and there stood the wife of
this man. She said, "In our tribe, when the wife goes away,
mother takes over." And so I lived with those people. And they
cared for me, fed me and looked after me. They did everything
that parents would do for a son. They taught me how to be a
missionary. I have never had such richness in relationships
that I had at that time, because I had so much to learn.

I share this incident with you, because I dearly wish that
anybody going to the mission field, would find it possible to
develop a close inter-personal relationship of that type. Not
for sentimentality sake, but to learn.

6. A Coping Strategy for processing new information and
experience in the face of culture shock. May I suggest to you
that if you do not give your missionary candidates some form of
cross-cultural preparation and orientation you neglect a pastoral responsibility to them. Five years down the road when the
chief executive officer visits the field, he will come back and
will say, "There's a concern about pastoral care among the
missionaries." I've heard it many times. The problem began back
at the beginning. Pastoral concern means giving to the people
the tools for coping. Usually 45% of the foreign students that
come to this country, return to their home country because of
what is called cultural shock. It needs definition and we are
not going to talk about that now. Those that remain are often
paralyzed by it even though they don't run away from it.
Another writer says, "Culture shock is a good teacher. It forces
the individual to consider alternatives and brings him to the
point of critically examining his personal concepts in the light
of new information providing he knows what to do with it." Teach
your missionaries what to do with new information and how to
process it and you will have people who are effective at least
twelve months earlier on the mission field. Without a coping
strategy culture shock will cause a person to defensively re-
inforce the familiar and fail to embrace innovation.

7. <u>A Servant Heart</u>. This has been expressed to us so often.
In my message at Winona Lake, I pointed out that the Lord gives
one of His most potent negative commandments in Matthew 20 when
He says, "But it shall not be so among you." And what He's
speaking about is top-down positions. He is pointing out how
the Gentiles do it. He indicates that some have top-down authority over others. He says that they exercise privileges that
other people don't have. They are over-lords. And then He says
you may not have it that way in the Body of Christ. And the
missionary of tomorrow, if he's to be effective, must know and
see modeled for him today that there are only peers in the
family of God. Different gifts, different roles, but no difference in status.

8. <u>A Willingness to Change</u>. To surrender rigidity for a
degree of flexibility which I have called sanctified compromise.
Compromise is frowned upon when we are thinking of compromising
the absolutes. But compromising things that are cultural and
surrendering things are biases are wholesome and realistic when
it comes to immersing ourselves in the lives of other people or
as Lee puts it in the novel, <u>To Kill a Mockingbird</u>, getting
inside a person's skin and walking around in it.

9. <u>A Solemn Sense of the Implications of the Incarnation
for Mission</u>. I wish that the paper this morning were on the
theology of incarnation, because here I think we have the answer
to that word which has eluded us for so long. The word "identification". We have asked ourselves should I wear the national
dress, should I eat the national food, should I sleep in the
national bed, and all of that. Then we mistakenly call that
identification. Our Lord; can you see Him surrounded with
splendor and glory, honor, adoration and praise; counted it not
a thing to be grasped at, but of His own volition gladly and
willingly becoming incarnate in flesh like yours and mine. And
you know the temptations of yesterday, don't you? He felt them.
True humanity. Very man, very God. I'm not suggesting that you
and I can be very man and very God, but I am suggesting that the
model of the incarnation is the essence of identification. We
become contextual in another culture only when we are incarnate
in that culture, and when we are modeling the very incarnation
of Jesus in our own lives. This is of the very essence of relevance. For God is always relevant. And to be relevant in our
generation in the place to which God is sending us, among the
people with whom we are going to live, we may have to change our
style in order to be relevant.

10. <u>An Awareness of the Church as the Whole People of God</u>.
Bishop Tucker writing in 1908 in a little paper called, "Toward
an Indigenous Church in Uganda", says that it is a contradiction

when a missionary is anything other than a member of the Body
of Christ. When he's outside the church, he is a constant reminder to those who are inside that what they are doing is merely
a sham. For if he thought it were worthwhile becoming a part
of it, he would be in it and identifying with it. If he cannot
be in it, then he is not of it, for it is not worth joining.
Therefore, the action is not really inside the church, but outside the church. Isn't that phenomenal? That was 1908 when
they knew where the action was. We somehow lost it in-between.
The missionary of tomorrow if he is to be effective in God is to
identify himself with those people who are in very truth the
people of God, to love them, to join them, and to be a part of
them. Personally, I don't see how a missionary can be anything
other than a member of the church, that is organically joined
as a member of the local assembly.

The third area of this first part of the paper is the
Necessary Skills which a missionary must acquire. I have tried
to group them into five areas. The first one is this -- A Knowledge of the Country. An intelligent awareness of what is going
on there. If we are to be effective for God, let us use and
exercise our intelligence. Let us be avid students of the news.
Let us be subscribers to scholarly journals which can at least
tune us into what the thinking of people is. For example, is
there a missionary executive here today who does not know that
popular opinion in Africa today is that Israeli action at
Entebbe was a violation of the rights of Uganda and feel bitterly
antagonistic toward the Israelis for it? Do you know that? Well
if you read Africa Magazine, you will discover that. We must
have an intelligent awareness of the political trends. How
many of us here would recommend for example, to a missionary
going to the Far East, that they study the "Thoughts of Mao Tse
Tung" which have had a great influence upon the thinking of
people? I am not holding them up as a model for you, I am merely
suggesting that you are going to meet people who think that way,
and it is a good idea to know why.

The second is Specific Skills for the Task. Obviously,
there are going to be the specifics of the task. If a person
is going to remove the appendix of someone, he must have received surgical preparation.

The third is Special Skills for Selected Ministry. For
example, you're recruiting a team and you're going to send them
into a city, and I'm excited about this concept of team ministry.
You are gathering together this group of people, and you have
taken a good cross-section and here they are all waiting for
orientation, and we ask, "what are you going to do?" Their
answer is, "Urban evangelism". Now, how many of you have sat at

the feet of Roger Greenway? How many of you have been to the
inner-city of Philadelphia, and studied with Harvie Conn in the
relationships that he is building there? How many of you have
been to see the AIM work in Newark, New Jersey? They all sit
there with their hands down, and say well we've never heard of
such a thing. I suggest dear brethren and missionary executives
that there are specialized skills which matter greatly in the
task to which God is calling us. We must have a responsible
attitude. By not properly orienting them at the initial point,
we lose some of their effectiveness over the first year or two.
Let us be innovative. If FEGC is doing a good thing, why not
send somebody from AIM to find out about it? Isn't that body
life, isn't that brotherly love, isn't that the fellowship of
which we've been speaking? If SIM has an interesting program
could they not share with OMS International? It isn't very
often that missionary executives say, "please help me." We don't
know how to do that in our missions.

Fourth, The Ability to Plan in response to stated organizational goals. Now would you please note the choice of words
there. I am a firm believer that the person who has the responsibility for carrying out objectives, ought to set them. Set
your missionary free to be himself and to be relevant in his
community, and to set objectives which are appropriate to that
community in the light of the goals that you describe as a
mission executive. Let me read a comment here from Lawrence
Goldberg. "In bureaucratic organizations there are a number of
shared expectations which mitigate against an individual assuming responsibility for the end of his actions." If you give
him his objectives and require him to follow through according
to your dictates that is what he will do.But he will be irrelevant in the community where he lives, because he is doing what
you tell him, not what he purposes to do. Also you provide for
him the most idle excuse in the book. The ability to plan is
very important.

Fifth, Experience in Evangelism and Nurture. I doubt if I
would be willing to send a missionary overseas without having
experienced the joy of having led a man or woman or a
young person to Jesus Christ, and of restoring backsliders. A
missionary must have a heart concern for those who are hurting
and demonstrate in tangible ways the fact that he cares about
people. If the evangelism of the world is committed to the
people of God, the missionary of tomorrow must be engaged with
a passion for men and women exposed to others, because that
is risky and because he will find the need for resources when
he does it. He will learn an awful lot about himself when he
is working one-on-one at that hostile university trying to
build a bridge of trust and get to know somebody better, so
that he can lead them to Jesus.

The second part of my paper is called Section B. The question which it addresses is this, "Where are these people, these missionaries of tomorrow whom God is calling into mission for tomorrow."

First, I believe that they are <u>Where We Have Traditionally Found Them</u>. In the Bible schools and colleges and seminaries and in the local church where we have traditionally as evangelical missions gone to look for them. I suggest therefore that the missionary be better prepared to understand the Third World man--his cultures, sociology, etc. This involves the responsibility of suggesting and requesting radical change in curriculum and methodology in various centers where missionaries are being trained. If that is where they are, brethren, then you and I have a solemn obligation to ascertain that the vital ingredients of missionary preparation, not only academically but experientially are incorporated in those schools which serve us. And I repeat, they do serve us, because they serve the body. Could we as executives of EFMA and IFMA give the AEPM (The Association of Evangelical Professors of Missions) an agenda item? Would it be possible for us to say to that agency, that organization, that fraternity, that we would wish them to form a study commission to work on what might be appropriate curricula for missionary education? Or shall we perpetuate the saber-toothed legend in our Bible schools, colleges, and seminaries where we may end up with a degree, but we may not end up with a relevant person for tomorrow's mission. Because the missionary of tomorrow is already there in those places, can missions, rather than recruit them, minister to them.

Howard Whaley who stood at this podium has told me many times of what it has meant to him to have been sought out by Virgil Newbrander who has helped him, encouraged him, loved him, and stood with him, until a friendship formed between an older and a younger man. And today there you have a man, professor of missions, in a well-known Bible college. God uses that kind of relationship. Are we ministry-oriented brethren, or are we looking for live warm bodies so that we can go back and tell the chief executive officer you have more candidates. So you got more people. Perhaps you may do them an injustice. Let us begin ministry to them now because we know where they are. A determined planned effort can rid missions of irrelevance in a short time just as we have rid our vocabulary of words which caused offense in society, within the last few years. We can demythologize missions. We can remove missions from the esoteric to the real if we want to. But brethren I fear in my spirit that we don't want to, because it is secure to live the missionary myth in an age of change.

The second location is on the <u>Non-Christian Campus</u>, the secular campus. I believe that there is a vast reservoir of resources gathered together on the university campus today. Now I want to ask you where are mission directors who care enough to get alongside them and minister to them. I'm not talking about recruiting them yet. By all means, recruit them, but not yet. Minister to them out of the perspective that you alone have as mission directors and missionaries. Get alongside them. Sit in the refectory and eat with them. Gather in their Bible studies. Be their friends and stop by whenever you're in town. The issue is a caring issue. Channel them first into mission before you channel them into missions. Set their hearts aglow with a flaming passion for men and women. Maybe they will become professionals and go overseas. They may never join a missionary society, but when they are out there they will say, you know I remember a conversation I had with this man or that man ten years ago on this campus at this time, and here I am. God was working. When you produce for your Board the list of schools you have visited as an executive and there isn't a secular campus among them, I ask you dear brethren, have you missed the mark? Because that is where the people are. I started with my first point, with people in the traditional places, but there are other people of God. And they are butting their heads against the obstacles at this point, and they're learning. They are already in cross-cultural encounter. They are already giving an account for their faith in a hostile environment. And that is something you can't always say about the theological seminary and other places like them. These are not preferable to others. I am not telling you that is where the best people are, but I am telling you that there are a lot of people there. Their training in life enhances their relevance for mission. I would suggest to you that the Christian on the secular campus that has learned how to cope with those remarkable differences in the sub-culture of America will have very little difficulty finding a basis for relationship in the Third World.

The third location, they are to be found in the <u>Ranks of Professionals</u> who are today waiting to be included in mission. Now by professionals I am meaning those who are in secular skills, trades, and professions. I am not using the term professional - non-professional missionary, I don't think it obtains. I am speaking about people who are waiting to be included who will not join a mission agency for God will not lead them there. Some of these are already overseas or they are planning to go. I am asking you brethren, will you join in an effort to maximize existing resources? I am not talking about a massive recruitment drive, just maximize what is. We have some tentative statistics. Somebody has said that there

will be a hundred and five other Americans overseas every year
for one missionary. We hope that there will be a percentage of
Christians among them. Somebody else has said seventeen percent
of all Americans will spend at least one year of their lives
overseas. There are those who would go overseas if to do so in
a secular role were to be regarded by the church as being mission
Do you follow my logic there? There are those who would go if
they felt that there was about it an encouragement from missions
and churches. Missions must acknowledge those people. Single
them out and recognize them. Form an associate branch, an arm,
a wing, a fellowship, a fraternity, and gather them in and include them and say to them, we love you and we think you are
just as much missionaries as our member missionaries. They are
going to have opportunities that some of our other people will
not have. We have talked about Saudi Arabia and places like
that where secular professionals are in and missionaries not so
successfully so. Intercristo has just recently asked Missionary
Internship to conduct a program with them next June to train
secular professionals for Christian service overseas. We are
going to do it, God helping us. Give the toll-free number of
Intercristo to people, get them to call in. There is training
for them, cross-cultural orientation. MAP International out of
Wheaton, are talking about exactly the same thing -- gathering
together resources in the family of God. Inter-Varsity has
been involved with this ministry for some time. They are still
doing it. Let us go on encouraging these people. And then in
the local congregation when you have a mission conference, here
is a suggestion. Why don't you suggest to the pastor that not
only should he have the missionary-of-the-week, not only should
he have the student-of-the-week, not only should he have the
serviceman-of-the-week in the bulletin, but let him have the
Christian professional overseas in the bulletin. I worship in
a church where we pray for our missionaries every Sunday morning,
and we have had men in professions working for the Ford Motor
Company, for example, overseas and I do not recall ever once
praying for them. They are every bit as much an extension of
the church overseas as those of us who were missionaries.

     The fourth location in which these people are to be found,
They Are Already in the Third World. They are among the Christians of the Third World. They are there and they are the
missionaries of tomorrow. You see, these are not just the personnel of the mission agency recruited in the North American
sub-continent, but they are the people of God, our peers, our
joint-heirs-with-Jesus, our friends and brethren. A missionary
is to be a reminder to mission wherever he is. Your missionaries
are there. Then can we not as we relate to the church of the
Third World encourage them in their outreach and when there are
those from within them who show a Luis Palau potential, incor-

porate them. Overseas Crusades are to be congratulated for
what they have done in nurturing a man who is now president of
the organization. Beautiful testimony of an inter-relationship
there. Not without its problems, because we have all kinds of
inter-cultural factors to consider, but the determination to do
it brought it about, and that is the exciting thing; including
nationals in missionary work. Why are we so afraid to incorporate nationals right within the mission itself? At the same
time where there is a genuine missionary movement within the
church of the Third World, let us cooperate there and help and
encourage. But please, brethren do not encourage nationals
of the Third World to structure a Third World mission like a
Western mission. Think of one-fortieth of your problems, and
don't propose a structure which will incorporate them. Lead
your national colleagues to structures which are viable within
the bounds of their own culture, because structures have values.
If they take your structure, they will take your values with it,
and they will emerge as a foreign organization. If you want the
evidence for that, look at the collection of Third World missions
that was published not very long ago. Just about every one
of them has a structure that is recognizable as Western. I don't
demean them. I applaud them for their dedication to mission. I
am concerned however that there were another three or four
hundred missions that never got in there, because they didn't
have a recognizable structure. Fifth, and finally, where are
these people to be found? They are among the Mature Men and
Women, chronologically mature, in our society. He offers
himself with the maturity of middle life, with having raised a
family, he knows what it is to have paid off a home or at least
gotten into that, he has had the struggle of running two or
three cars because his children were growing up and rushing
hither and yon and he had to get to the office. He has been in
the rough and tumble of counseling with clients. He knows what
people are all about. He knows how to gauge his senses in a
changing world. And as Akira Hatori said to me on one occasion,
"he comes to us with immediate usefulness, and then he said if
you send us the boys, we will have to train them." You and I
avidly get into the high schools and the colleges, and so we
must. But would you not believe that out there in the great
population of the churches of North America are men and women
who say, "am I on the garbage heap of God's family?" And then
they get in their car the next morning being Monday, and they
open their office door and on its label is written Vice-President, Senior Executive Officer, Consultant, Medical Doctor, etc.
And somebody said if you're past 30 you can't be a missionary.
This is nonsense. The mature judgment of a man in middle life
is a tremendous asset in the mission of the church today. Do
not question the availibility of the man in mature years. It
may be that the missionary that joins you at 45 can give you

twenty years. It's very unlikely that the missionary who joins
you at 25 will be with you at 45 today. These are the pressures
of society. People are not committing themselves for long-term
service like they used to. With a reduction in long-term
commitment among younger people, with the economic pressures
that are going to be brought to bear upon this country in the
future, these people may be the answer to a very important need.

I'm grateful for your attention. I realize that this is
only scratching the surface of a very large subject. But it
is exciting to think that there are going to be people in the
mission of the church tomorrow, and I believe that they are
going to be people whom we know, and with whom we will have the
privilege of working.

10

MISSIONS AND THE FUTURE

by Ian M. Hay

Our theme for this week of meetings reminds me of a Chinese proverb: "To prophesy is extremely difficult - especially with respect to the future!"

The theme was well chosen. We have listened to our national brethren - carefully; we have discussed with them the future role of missions. We have listened to ourselves - perhaps less carefully! We have thought of the issues and patterns. We have talked of finance and education. Of management - evangelism and personnel.

What's left? My task is to speak on missions and the future. After all of that I have a formidable task indeed.

We who stand on the threshold of the last quarter of this century do well to try to project ourselves into the future, but let's remember that no serious futurist deals in prediction. Apart from biblical revelation we are not able to speak with precision and certainty about the future.[1] We have no crystal ball, and even with the wisdom of the Holy Spirit, God has not seen fit to give us today what Dr. Clowney once called a pocket-sized Urim and Thummin.

Top Management expert Peter Drucker warns:

"Planning also suffers from the illusion that computers and systems will insure certain success. This is ridiculous; no one can foresee the future. True,

---

Ian M. Hay, presently General Director of the Sudan Interior Mission, was born of missionary parents in Nigeria and worked as a missionary in Africa where he became Field Secretary before taking up duties in the U.S. headquarters.

> strategic planning, although nothing new in itself,
> does have new tools and techniques at its disposal,
> but it would be a mistake to rely on these too whole-
> heartedly - some of the best planning has been done
> on the back of an envelope. Strategic planning
> definitely does not substitute facts for judgment,
> substitute science for the manager, or eliminate
> risk. Rather, it enables management to choose the
> right risk to carry out a course of action that can
> be changed to meet change, to slough off yesterday
> through planned abandonment of the past."[2]

The last sentence puts in a nutshell our role as mission executives, choose the right action to meet change and slough off yesterday through planned abandonment of the past.

Toffler, in his impressive, although thoroughly secular book, Future Shock says that "Previously men studied the past to shed light on the present. I Have turned the time mirror around convinced that a coherent image of the future can only shower us with valuable insight into today".[3]

We are to do the same. After all, eschatology is history from God's perspective.

Probably the thing that strikes us most urgently about the future is summed up in the word "change". We have heard a lot about that, haven't we? And well we should. "Change" Toffler tells us "is avalanching upon our heads, and most people are grotesquely unprepared to cope with it."[4]

By way of example, Buckminster Fuller says that in 1911 the typical American averaged 1,640 miles per year of total travel containing 1,300 miles of just everyday walking to and fro. This means that he traveled only 340 miles per year with the aid of a horse or a mechanical means.

How far did you travel last year? Well, we are all abnormal, aren't we? I have come close to 100,000 miles all told in the last 12 months. The average American, however, while not doing that much, does do 10,000 miles per year.

I am always amazed on every African flight I make to ride on a full plane of traveling Africans. A fast pace is part of our milieu.

Missionaries have and do face culture shock. We've dis-cussed this phenomenon for years, but future shock is a sick-ness that will affect not only missionaries in the coming days, but mission leaders in particular.

By definition Toffler who coined the term says that it is "the shattering stress and disorientation we induce in individuals by subjecting them to too much change in too short a time."[6]

Missions in the future face this problem.

The trouble is that too many of us are like the Duke of Cambridge who said "any change at any time for any reason is to be deplored" or like the poet who said: "Come weal, come woe, My status is quo."

What is this change that faces us? Again to quote Toffler, he says that

> "Change is the process by which the future invades our lives and it is important to look at it clearly, not merely from the grand perspectives of history, but also from the vantage point of the living, breathing individuals who experience it."[7]

Our task for the future then is not to try to halt change. That can't be done. Our task is to find ways to manage it in our service for our Lord Jesus Christ.

Twenty-one years ago Harold Lindsell published his *Missionary Principles and Practices*. At the conclusion of that book, he said,

> "What of the future? This is a final word. Yet it cannot be final because the future belongs to God, and what men say is but a guess. Limited to imperfect knowledge of the past and without great insight into the future, man can peer dimly into that dark glass and plot pathways conjecturally. Time will tell how accurately he has diagnosed situations and how well the panaceas suggested have worked. The Christian in this otherwise obscure dimness, has a peculiar advantage over most others. Whereas he enters into that which is unknown to him, it is known to God. The believer need have no fear of that which is unknown to him because he realizes that the future is God's and that his ally, God, will see him through, and he will ever be the God of history completing His eternal purposes for man.

"The Church of Jesus Christ is living between the
time - between the time of its creation and the
time of its consummation. It lives in tension
as a witness to the grace of God so that its very
nature presupposes it will plan for and enter into
the future with the expectation its work will be
needed until the end of history. The Church must
have its plans ready and its sight set."[8]

Did you catch it? "The very nature of the Church presupposes that it will plan for and enter into the future with
the expectation that its work will be needed until the end of
history." That's precisely what missions in the future is all
about. Isaiah questioned God about this. When he joyously
responded to God's request for a worker, he was stunned to find
he was commissioned to a failing task - to harden men's hearts;
to make their ears heavy and their eyes dim. He said how long
do I keep that up? God replied, "Until the cities are wasted
without inhabitant". In other words till it's all over.(Is. 6)

What's it like then to be a Christian missionary in the
last quarter of the 20th century? May I submit that, for all
of our projections this week, there is nothing new under the
sun. We are just like our first century counterparts. One of
them put it this way: "We are troubled on every side, yet not
distressed; we are perplexed but not in despair; persecuted,
but not forsaken; cast down, but not destroyed; always bearing
about in the body the dying of the Lord Jesus, that the life
also of Jesus might be made manifest in our body." (II Cor.
4:8, 9)

In my travels this last year I have become impressed more
than ever with what God is doing. Personal observations shows
me that the Holy Spirit is at work. People are being saved.
The Church is growing around the world. Christians are
acknowledging the Lordship of Christ. Our prayer times this
week have emphasized this point.

Such blessing, however, does not come easily. There is
an African proverb, "Even the most beautiful fig may have a
worm in it." From my own perspective in SIM, I notice that
African Christians and missionaries alike are faced with
fresh problems daily. Satanic pressures and persecutions are
the norm. It is a strange kind of persecution, however, -
nothing exotic. Missionaries are not tied to the stake or put
in boiling pots these days. It all seems much more ordinary.
Some are accused falsely and required to spend endless hours
before magistrates. Others are held hostage in situations
approaching anarchy. Still others are attacked physically, not

because of their Christian commitment, but simply because they
are caught between violent forces. It might be easier if the
problems did come because of their stand for the faith. They
would know what to do then. Ordinary or not, the pressure is
there, and it is enormous. Remember, driver ants pick a carcass
cleaner than does a lion.

It's not an easy time, and my projection for missions in
the future is that it will get worse. What reaction then will
missions and Christians in general have to these rapidly changing circumstances, to physical danger? There are no simplistic
answers. Circumstances and times differ. On one occasion Paul
decided simply to escape in a basket let down over a wall.
What ignominy. In talking about this Paul said, "If I must
boast I will boast of the things that show my weakness...In
Damascus the governor under King Aretas had the city of
Damascenes guarded in order to arrest me, but I was lowered in
a basket from a window in a wall and slipped through his hands."
(II Cor. 11:30 - 33)

On a different occasion Paul headed right into the danger
in spite of clear advice from friends and sure knowledge from
the Holy Spirit that prison and hardships faced him.(Acts 20:23)
In one instance he avoided the danger. In the other he met it
head-on.

We must not be foolhardy nor capricious. At times for
the good of the Church and for his own sake, a missionary
must leave. That comes not from cowardice but from godly
wisdom.

On the other hand, leaving a situation does not mean
freedom from problems. One of our missionaries was challenged
recently by an African Christian who reminded him that you can't
escape from difficulty by fleeing. "If you run away from
difficulty," he said, "where is the victory? Where is the
crown?"

In a very real sense, the times demand that each wait on
the Lord for his own answer for the situation in which he finds
himself.

We must not be surprised at anything that happens to us in
coming days. We have to be like the Psalmist who said, "Surely
he shall not be moved forever: the righteous shall be in everlasting remembrance. He shall not be afraid of evil tidings:
His heart is fixed, trusting in the Lord. His heart is established, he shall not be afraid." (Ps. 112:6-8)

Two hundred years ago in the agonies of the war for American independence Thomas Paine wrote that "Summer soldiers and sunshine patriots will not in this crisis come to the aid of their country." So in the future Christ's soldiers have to learn that to be in His Army involves more than dress uniforms, victory parades or gigantic costly conferences. It takes those who can in truth "endure hardness as good soldiers" on the cutting edge of his enterprise.

Suffering is not to be avoided. As we serve Christ we must learn that our surrender to His Lordship which puts us where we are is unconditional. If He puts any of us in the midst of adversity, we have to continue to live as unto the Lord. We have to rest assured that what is committed to Christ is well cared for.

All of these problems shouldn't cause us alarm. Our Commander gave us fair warning that trouble would come. As I have already mentioned, Paul faced similar problems. By God's grace we today will respond as he did.

Recently writing in Evangelical News Letter Dr. T. Christie Wilson spoke of the closed doors around the world and said,

> "How are those in closed countries going to hear the Gospel? It will be through rededicating ourselves to the completion of Christ's mission, through all the means at our disposal, through the mobilization all over the world for evangelism, through fervent prayer and through the directing and empowering of the Holy Spirit. In Acts 12 we read, 'Prayer was made without ceasing of the Church unto God...and. ...the iron gate which led into the city...opened.. ..automatically.'[9]

This morning, like Mark Anthony, I can only say, "I am but a plain, blunt man. I speak the things that you yourselves do know". Therefore, without any hesitancy I refer you in these closing moments of our session together to a most familiar passage – John 20:19 – 23.

> "On the evening of that first day of the week, when the disciples were together, with the doors locked for fear of the Jews, Jesus came and stood among them and said, "Peace be with you!" After he said this, He showed them His hands and side. The disciples were overjoyed when they saw the Lord.

Again Jesus said, 'Peace be with you! As the Father
has sent me so send I you' and with that He breathed
on them and said 'Receive the Holy Spirit. If you
forgive anyone his sins they are forgiven. If you
do not forgive them they are not forgiven'."

John Stott in his challenging new book, "Christian Mission
in the Modern World" says that

"The crucial form in which the Great Commission has
been handed down to us (though it is the most neglected because it is the most costly) is the
Johanine. Jesus had anticipated it in His prayer
in the upper room when He said to the Father: 'As
thou hast sent me into the world, so I have sent
them into the world,' (John 17:18) Now, probably
in the same upper room but after His death and
resurrection He turned His prayer statement into
a commission and said: 'As the Father has sent
me even so I send you.' (John 20:21) In both these
sentences Jesus did more than draw a vague parallel
between His mission and ours. Deliberately and precisely He made His mission the model of ours, saying,
as the Father sent me, so send I you. Therefore,
our understanding of the church's mission must be
deduced from our understanding of the Son's. Why
and how did the Father send the Son?" [10]

It was the first Easter. The disciples were gathered together out of fear of the Jews. This was their first assembly.
The parallel passage of Luke 24 tells us that it was the disciples and the others. We don't know exactly how many were
there. It could have been as many as 120.

But fear clutched at their hearts. This was characteristic
of them, and it was understandable. They were weak. Their
Master was dead. They had much to fear.

So despair gripped their hearts as well. Their future was
dark and forbidding. To top it all, they doubted. Luke 24 and
Mark 16 reveal their attitude.

"And their words seemed to them as idle tales, and
they believed them not."

"Oh, fools, and slow of heart to believe all that the
prophets have spoken."

We can empathize with these first century Christians. Our
world faces the same collapse.

But then Jesus came, "And while they yet believed not for joy and wondered...." (Luke 24:41)

"One glimpse of His dear face
All sorrow did erase."

And Jesus showed them His hands and His side. They were strengthened. The realization of the resurrected Christ standing in their presence transformed their dense darkness to glowing light.

Peter Marshall said, "resurrection never becomes a fact of experience until the living Christ lives in the heart of the believer."

And He said, PEACE. Here is the fulfillment of John 14:27. "Peace I leave with you; my peace I give you. I do not give to you as the world gives. Do not let your hearts be troubled and do not be afraid."

His dual "shalom" took the disciples from personal greeting to a message of depth. The first was the eastern form of greeting - good evening. The second was what they needed.

To troubled, discouraged Christians Jesus appeared. He came to commission them, but before he did, He gave them Himself and spoke peace to their hearts.

What faces missions in the future? Who knows? But if we are to be effective servants of Jesus Christ we need a fresh realization of His resurrection power and life; we need to have His peace and joy flooding our souls. Nothing is more contrary to God's will than frustrated troubled Christians scurrying around trying to witness for Him.

One day one of our missionaries was witnessing to a Muslim. He emphasized the historic fact of the resurrection of Christ. He contrasted the living Christ to a dead prophet. The Muslim challenged him, "And what does your living Jesus do for you that my dead Mohammed does not do for me?" We better know experientially the answer to that question.

Then Jesus challenged them with his commission -- a simple phrase. There is nothing difficult about it. There are no polysyllabics. Even a child can understand the meanings of the words. Yet how pregnant these words are. "As the Father hath sent me, even so send I you."

Here is the purpose of God for all ages. It's there in its totality. And that's what missions are for the future.

Jesus came into the world to reveal the Father. He shared the Father's pity and concern for the world and, sent by the Father, He came to show the Father. The disciples could say "we have seen and do testify that the Father sent the Son to be the Saviour of the world. (I John 4:9,10,14)

Stott says:

"So He gave Himself in selfless service for others and His service took a wide variety of forms according to men's needs. Certainly He preached, proclaiming the good news of the Kingdom of God and teaching about the coming and the nature of the Kingdom, how to enter and how it would spread. But He served in deed as well as in word, and it would be impossible in the ministry of Jesus to separate His works from His words. He fed hungry mouths and washed dirty feet, He healed the sick, comforted the sad and even restored the dead to life."[11]

Jesus exemplified the love of God which evidenced itself in pity for the world.

The prophets spoke of this. Isaiah speaking of God's hatred of pollution said,

"The earth is defiled under the inhabitants thereof; because they have transgressed the laws, changed the ordinances, broken the everlasting covenant." (Isa. 24:5)

Again he said,

"Is such a fast that I have chosen a day for a man to afflict his soul? Is it to bow down his head as a bulrush and to spread sackcloth and ashes under him? Wilt thou call that a fast, and an acceptable day of the Lord? Is not this the fast that I have chosen? To loose the bands of wickedness, to undo the heavy burdens, and to let the oppressed go free, and that you break every yoke? Is it not to deal thy bread to the hungry, and that thou bring the poor that are cast out to thy house? When thou seest the naked that thou cover him; and that thou hide not thyself from thine own flesh? (Isa. 58:5-7)

The Psalmist said,

"Happy is he that hath the God of Jacob for his help,
whose hope is in the Lord his God' which made heaven
and earth, the sea and all that therein is: which
keepeth truth forever: which executeth judgment
for the oppressed: which giveth food for the hungry,
the Lord looseth the prisoners; the Lord openeth
the eyes of the blind: the Lord raiseth up them
that are bowed down: the Lord loveth the righteous:
the Lord preserveth the strangers; He relieveth the
fatherless and widows, but the way of the wicked
He turns upside down." (Psalm 140:6)

And Jesus came with those same concerns. In His home town
synagogue early in His ministry He picked up the scroll of
Isaiah and read, "the Spirit of the Lord God is upon me; because
the Lord hath anointed me to preach good tidings to the meek;
He hath sent me to bind up the broken hearted, to proclaim
liberty to the captives and the opening of the prison to them
that are bound; to proclaim the acceptable year of the Lord."
(Isaiah 60:1) And that day the sermon was short, "This day is
this scripture fulfilled in your ears." Matthew tells us that
He "went into all the cities and villages teaching in their
synagogues and preaching the gospel of the Kingdom, healing every
sickness and every disease among the people, but when He saw the
multitudes He was moved with compassion on them because they
fainted and were scattered abroad as sheep having no shepherd."
(Matthew 9:35,36) That deep compassion took Him to the cross.

We have the same responsibility. God's purpose, like His
character is immutable. We are to go as He came. Let's not
forget that the only way that God could communicate with us was
for the Eternal Word to become flesh or as Kenneth Strachan said,
"The Foreign Word has to become indigenous flesh." And now
Jesus is gone. He sends us with the same compassion - the same
pity - to do the same thing. We are now to be the foreign word
in His world; our task is to become indigenous flesh.

We must communicate that Word.
We are light; we must arise and shine!
We are salt. What a catastrophe if it loses its savor!

He showed compassion on the hungry. So must we.
He taught. So must we.
He reconciled men to God; "we stand in His stead
   beseeching men today to be reconciled to God".

An overwhelming task. How can we do it? The only possible
way is to go in the same manner that He came. Again Stott
reminds us "Now He sends, He says, as the Father had sent Him.
Therefore, our mission, like His, is to be one of service. He
emptied Himself of status, took the form of a servant, and His
humble mind is to be in us. (Phil. 2:5-8) He supplies us with
the perfect model of service, and sends His Church into the
world to be a servant Church."[12]

Peering into the future, we feel like a weak, frail bark
in the midst of a fierce storm; like broken reeds scarcely
held together. Yet the truth is that all the powers of hell
cannot crush us. The gates of hell cannot prevent the building
of His Church. He has given us the dynamic to do what He told
us to. In verse 22 it says He breathed on them. Once before
He breathed. It was on Adam, and he became a living soul. Now
He breaths the very breath of God and ordains new life with all
of God's power. The breathing was symbolic in the same way the
prophets used symbols to show a truth. This was the earnest
and not many days hence the power of the Holy Spirit came upon
the first century Christians. They learned that power is a
Person.

The late Dr. Tozer constantly warned us that in evangelicalism there is a danger. Too often we stand like the priests
piling up stones, laying on wood on the altar, all of which is
worthless without fire from above. He said, "In all thy
getting get unction." One perceptive spiritual national said
that the thing they needed most from missionaries is not
technical expertness, but a person with missionary passion who
can communicate that passion to the church. Again I say
nothing new. Missions of the future must utilize Spirit filled
people empowered by God. Men who cry:

> "Breathe on me breath of God.
> Fill me with life anew
> That I may love what thou dost love
> And do what thou wouldst do.
>
> Breathe on me breath of God
> Till I am wholly thine
> Till all this earthly part of me
> Glows with Thy power divine.

Again Stott says, "And now He sends us 'into the world' to
identify with others as He identified with us (though without
losing our Christian identity) to become vulnerable as He did.
It is surely one of the most characteristic failures of us
Christians, not least of us who are called evangelical Christians,

that we seldom seem to take seriously this principle of incarnation....It comes more natural to us to shout the gospel at people from a distance than to involve ourselves deeply in their lives, to think ourselves into their culture, their problems and to feel with them in their pains."[13] The message we proclaim is of forgiveness of sins. He came to take away the sins of the world; we are to proclaim it. If we do and men receive it their sins are forgiven and if we don't do it, and therefore, men do not hear, their sins are still on them. This is what verse 23 is all about. We have the glorious privilege of declaring to all men everywhere that their sins have been forgiven as they put their trust in our Lord and Saviour Jesus Christ. We have also the solemn authority in the power of the Holy Spirit to those rejecting Christ to declare that their sins are retained or still upon them. We bring men to a crisis so that they can either make Him Lord of their lives or join at the foot of the cross shouting "Crucify Him". Each person hearing that witness must make a choice.

The task for the future is clear. Let's do it with dedication of purpose. Let's be constant and have our priorities where they ought to be. Let's get on with the task.

"So send I you to labor unrewarded
    To serve unfamed, unloved, unsought, unknown
To bear rebuke; to suffer scorn and scoffing
    So send I you to toil for Me alone.

"So send I you to bind the bruised and broken,
    O'er wandering souls to work, to weep, to wake;
To bear the burdens of a world that's weary,
    So send I you to suffer for My sake.

"So send I you to leave your life's ambition
    To die to dear desire: self-will resign;
To labor lone and love where men revile;
    So send I you to lose your life in mine.

"So send I you to hearts made hard by hatred
    To eyes made blind because they will not see
To spend, though be it hard to spend and spare not
    So send I you to taste of Calvary."

As the Father hath sent me, so send I you.

NOTES FOR CHAPTER 10

1. Alvin Toffler, <u>Future Shock</u>, New York, Random House, Inc.,
    1970, pp. 6, 7.

2. Peter Drucker, On Management, New York AMACOM, Audio
    Cassette No. 1, 1974.

3. Alvin Toffler, <u>op.cit.</u> p. 5.

4. <u>Ibid</u>. p. 14.

5. <u>Ibid</u>., p.69

6. <u>Ibid</u>., p.4

7. <u>Ibid</u>., p.3

8. Harold Lindsell, <u>Missionary Principles and Practices</u>
    Westwood, N.J., Fleming H. Revell Co., 1955, p. 355.

9. Christie T. Wilson, <u>Evangelical News Letter</u>, Philadelphia,
    PA, Evangelical Foundation, 1976.

10. John R.W. Stott, <u>Christian Mission in the Modern World</u>,
    Downers Grove, Illinois, Intervarsity Press, 1975, p.23.

11. <u>Ibid</u>., p.24

12. <u>Ibid</u>.

13. <u>Ibid</u>.

11
THE BEHAVIORAL SCIENCES AND
CHRISTIAN MISSION

by Marvin K. Mayers

The subject of this paper is so vast and the implications so extensive that I must limit myself severely. Thus you will find this is more of an outline than a discourse; more of a survey than an exhaustive treatment; more a guide than an argument. I trust that the Holy Spirit of God will open our eyes to the fascinating and exciting challenges we have as Christians to take many of the insights of the behavioral sciences and harness them to mission even as we have the insights of the discipline of theology.

As a young teen, I experienced salvation from sin through Jesus Christ. I was mentally, emotionally and spiritually confused and I found in Christ, through His Spirit, answers to life's deepest problems. I feel that the Spirit, as an outgrowth of that conversion and through Christian growth and maturity, led me to study social anthropology following one term of missionary service in Central America. I had then what I term a second conversion, a behavioral sciences conversion. I had been educated in college as an historian and in seminary as a theologian. Following that training and preparation, I went to the mission field and encountered problems for which I had no solutions, nor preparation to discover solutions. I had theological problems but many of the challenges I faced were not theological ones.

Studying in my various classes in anthropology, in the behavioral sciences, in communication, in social relations and social structure I began to see how I could cope with many of

Marvin K. Mayers, presently Director of the Summer Institute of Linguistics at Dallas and adjunct Professor of Linguistics at the University of Texas, Arlington, worked for 13 years in Guatemala under Wycliffe Bible Translators and then eight years as Professor of Anthropology at Wheaton. He has an M.Div. degree from Fuller, and M.A. and Ph.D. from the University of Chicago and is the author of *Christianity Confronts Culture, A Look at Latin American Lifestyles,* and joint author of *Reshaping Evangelical Higher Education.*

the problems I had previously faced in the field. I now had
alternative possibilities for dealing with them. I eagerly
returned to the field and found that what I had to communicate,
namely the Gospel of Jesus Christ, was more sound and deeply
meaningful than ever and the means I had to communicate this
tremendous truth were far more effective than previously.

I began to realize that:

Theology speaks to the WHAT TO communicate, which is
the truth of God in Christ.

Behavioral sciences speak to the HOW TO communicate
that truth in whatever linguistic-ethnic group.

Theology is the man-to-God and God-to-man relationship developed.

Behavioral science is the man-to-self and man-to-
man relationship developed -- all under the influence
and guidance of the Holy Spirit of God.

Thus my preparation for multicultural mission was not complete until I was trained in both theology and behavioral
sciences.

It is important when utilizing insights from the behavioral
sciences to know what behavioral sciences are not as well as
what they are, so that these insights may be used with confidence. The behavioral sciences are:

1. NOT a new teaching. They are not there to change
truth. They provide a different mindset, not a different faith.
They are a variation of culture, thus an educational subculture,
not a new creed.

2. NOT in competition with theology nor with doctrine.
They aid in the communication of sound theology and doctrine.

3. NOT the exclusive domain of scholars. (They are being
used at an increasing rate by Christian organizations within our
tradition: in publications, in small group guidance, in
counseling, in the training and preparation of missionary recruits, and in course work in Christian colleges and seminaries.)

4. NOT "behaviorism" of the teachings and traditions of
Skinner and Watson. These teachings derive from the physical
sciences and deal with determinism. The behavioral sciences
are, rather, fully within the social sciences and deal with

social control, fully compatible with the doctrine of free will.

5. NOT the "world system" ruled by Satan and his angels. Rather the behavioral sciences deal with cultural systems, given to man by God to provide law and order in the day by day experiences of life, and also as vehicles for knowing God fully and deeply.

On the other hand, the behavioral sciences _are_:

1. An academic discipline on a par with the humanities and physical sciences.

2. Primarily studies in the specific disciplines of anthropology, psychology, and sociology, but also in political science and economics. They are influencing much of what is being done today in management, education, architecture, and related disciplines.

3. The study, through sound research techniques, of human behavior wherever it is found. Such study is designed not to supplant God's truth, rather, to enhance it in the lives of men.

4. A fresh and vital way of looking at the Bible. 1) Role theory, stratification, space relationships and many other concerns of the behavioral sciences come to life in the Biblical scenes. 2) Role theory, for example helps us understand why even the king in the Old Testament would go into center city in sackcloth and ashes to confess personal sin and ask forgiveness. We do not make such a dramatic entrance into the public arena as did the Old Testament leaders, yet we can confess personal sin and find forgiveness even as they.

5. A fresh and vital way of looking at life. Concepts such as identity, self acceptance, adapting to culture all permit me freedom within the context of my culture.

In spite of an understanding of what the behavioral sciences are not, and a renewed insight into what they are and can be, many Christians are wary of the behavioral sciences. There are several reasons for this attitude.

1. Adherents and scholars of the behavioral sciences use a dialect of English different from that of the humanities in which one encounters the studies of theology, philosophy and the arts. Such language and dialect differences cause one to misunderstand what is being said. Christians, for example, are discovering value in the teachings of Carl Jung, the noted psychologist, which they previously overlooked. The dialect of

the behavioral sciences sounds at first, very secular. For example, the Bible says, "forgetting those things which are behind..." and the equivalent term in the behavioral sciences is "accept your past." You cannot begin to forget what lies in your past until you accept it wholly. Then the bad, useless, unwanted, is forgotten and the useful and good comes to our continued aid. The two ways of referring to this same concept make them sound like opposites when they are in reality the same.

2. Many behavioral scientists <u>have</u> repudiated sound Christianity and have nothing to do with the Bible. But the same is true of theologians and philosophers.

3. Liberals began using the terminology and concepts of the behavioral sciences before the fundamentalists and evangelicals began to discover their validity and use. But there can be sound Biblical behavioral scientists, even as there can be sound Biblical theologians, and there are and have been for decades.

4. Management used these concepts, principles and practices long before many in our tradition became fully aware of them, so the average Christian encountered them first in the business world. (For those whose world-and-life-view calls for a complete separation between the sacred and the secular, it was difficult to work with such concepts in the church. For them the behavioral sciences have little to do with the spiritual life. At the same time, this is one of the principal encouragements the behavioral sciences give the Christian living a Bible- Christ-centered life. God seeks to deal with the whole person in ways that will allow the Spirit to enter each aspect of life and renew and fulfill it.)

I have dealt, at some length, on a definition of the behavioral sciences, seeking to indicate in a variety of ways just what they are and what they are not. I wanted this noted body of Christian teachers to be very sure of what I feel can be utilized in Christian mission throughout the world.

The behavioral scientist can serve mission in the following ways: as counselor, consultant, trainer, communicator, educator, translator and researcher.

The <u>counselor</u> in Christian mission is more than a psychologist or a "shrink". He integrates Scriptures and his knowledge of human behavior in order to deal with issues and problems often unique to missionaries. People, even in mission, have personal conflict that calls for professional help. Every mission I know of makes use of such help when there is a serious problem too great for the mission executive to handle. We are finding in Wycliffe, as our own counseling department develops, that many people are helped tremendously by a brief visit or a short series of visits with a counselor. These people might not need long term professional counseling as some do, but need someone to talk to in resolving personal problems such as the loss of a loved one, some matter of guilt, or a source of personal insecurity. The counselor makes available to the entire mission useful readings, meaningful studies and spiritual growth material. The counseling department also initiates small sharing groups that get people talking together about the deeper things of life --people who would not have this opportunity short of some formalized arrangement. Every administrator is also being trained to be more aware of the people with whom they work, and living and working conditions in the entire mission are becoming more personally and spiritually fulfilling.

The counselor, trained in the area of marriage and family counseling has aided husbands and wives to reduce interpersonal conflict: to resolve, in briefer periods of time, conflicts that formerly hindered for lengthy periods their effective ministry, and to increase contact with their children -- reducing tension with their teenagers especially.

The counselor aids in resolving group conflict. I have been present in the business meetings of two evangelical missions during which participants literally yelled at each other over some matter each felt important at the time but which, upon further reflection, was most minor. The counselor builds into the very fabric of the mission program human relations training, interpersonal communication training, social psychology insights; and people find others more enriching and are able to make more positive use of the commands of Scripture to "love one another".

The peoples of the world find themselves displaced so frequently in these days due to war, earthquakes or famine, or just plain seeking personal or family betterment. The counselor as a social worker, cooperating fully with the missionary, can reach into homes and prepare such displaced and alienated people for the entrance of the Gospel and the ministry of the church in their lives.

The consultant has three primary responsibilities. He assists the missionary to know the people: how the people speak and how they live, interact and react. He further makes the missionary aware of new and fresh insights that can be brought to bear in mission: "others do it this way, and it works". How rewarding it is to pass on such insight and find the defeated missionary rejuvenated and renewed in hope. As an educator, I shared insights with a missionary who had literally given up hope. Later he couldn't wait to return to teach his people.

Finally, the consultant serves as "critic". By his trained objectivity he shares, "this is what you are doing, are you aware of its adverse side effects? Is this what you intend to do?"

Another time I studied the feuding pattern of a group of peoples related to each other through the past centuries. These people formed two-man feuds that endured until there was physical separation in death or geographical separation by moving. In sharing this pattern of feuding with the staff of a noted mission, the participants grew sullen and refused to hear more. The realization had come to each of them that every member of the mission had an on-going feud with some member of their church or community. As missionaries they had turned off the people rather than attracted them to their Lord, not a pleasing thought.

The trainer-orienter is one kind of educator. His role is to master a skill and then pass it on to the next person who is then trained effectively in the skill as well as trained to turn around and train the next. Probably the most useful expression of this is the master-apprentice relationship. This is not the characteristic educational challenge of the classroom, rather, the training program takes place where the skill is needed. In missions it is the challenge of the trainer to communicate and train one in his skill through culturally relevant ways. In the Philippines, an experienced pastor assumed the responsibility for a number of novice pastors. He attracted them to the ministry, provided them a mission church, guided their formal and informal education and encouraged each one of them to continue the process wherever they found themselves. The reverse of the above experience was a young man who spoke one language but who was trained in a Bible Institute in which a second language was spoken. This young man returned to his own area preaching sermons in the other language and using the forms and expressions of the other life style. He was obviously a misfit in his own area and his ministry suffered.

The trainer, as orienter/orientator is particularly useful in preparing short termers or full termers for the mission field and re-orienting them upon their return to their own country and culture. While I was at Wheaton, I became involved in the

Summer Mission project, a program sending from 12 to 45 young
people into the mission field for a summer missionary experience.
When I first associated with the program, I discovered that about
half of the young people were returning from the field having had
a bad experience -- they wanted no more to do with missions.
After working with Dr. Lindberg, now at Westmont, and Dr. Norton
of Wheaton, and introducing behavioral sciences training along
with the more recognized spiritual preparations as Bible study,
we found that the percentage of bad experiences began to decrease
and within a few years had become only one bad experience in 40.

The <u>communicator</u> becomes aware that there is more than one
part of a message being communicated. All messages carry at
least the verbal/vocal and the non-verbal associated with ges-
ture, facial expression, distance, position, etc. How easy it
is for us to tell our children we're listening yet communicate
to them by our look, the positioning of a newspaper, or such
like that we are deeply engrossed in something else and have not
heard a word they have said. One particularly critical inter-
change in missions came when I was accompanying my neighbor up
the mountain. We stopped to rest just as the sun was rising
over the eastern mountain. I reacted strongly to his saying,
"Here comes our father," in reference to the sun. I proceeded
to give him a science lecture of how the earth revolves around
the sun, and then ended most emphatically with the statement,
"Besides, God is our Father, it is He who made the sun and the
earth." I was totally unaware of his reaction, not realizing for
many years why he began to grow cool toward me and refuse to
hear my "good news". I had inadvertently communicated, in that
culture setting, that I both rejected him as a person and also
rejected his beliefs. I now know I can communicate acceptance
of a person even though I do not accept, or believe his point
of view. I can now relate to others behaviorally in the way I
was told God related to them -- He loves the sinner, yet hates
the sin. Having dynamic truth, yet failing as a communicator
of that truth I alienated my friend who I coveted as a brother
in Christ. What good is the soundest theology or doctrine if
we are unable to communicate these effectively to all people?

Some missionaries are natural communicators. I received
my behavioral sciences training which helped me work more
effectively in the field. My colleague and associate Harry
McArthur needed none of my formal training -- he was a natural
communicator. On the other hand, two young men went into an
underdeveloped nation and founded a university. Within just a
very few years they both returned to the States -- their inability to communicate produced too much tension for them to
continue. They could have benefited by extensive training in
multicultural communication.

The educator has a broader task than the trainer-orienter, yet a more specific task than the communicator. Whereas the trainer concentrates on the training in a skill and teaching of that skill to another, the educator has broader interests and seeks to educate larger numbers of students. The communicator is interested in communicating any message whereas the educator is selective of message as well as of the receptor of that message.

Adult education is not part of the American educational preparation yet many of the societies of the world are stratified on the basis of age -- the older one is, the more his people listen to him. If the missionary is not educated in adult education with crosscultural implications he is more likely to select and educate youths for the ministry than older men. In such societies these young men, trained as pastors, take twenty to forty years before they can truly lead their people, or are seen by them as leaders -- thus delaying the spread of the Gospel.

The educator also controls the subject matter of knowledge. Whereas the Bible is translated into hundreds of languages, speakers of those languages responding to it as "God is speaking my language", much theology taught in Bible schools and seminaries overseas is Western based theology. In my opinion, no theological issue should be resolved until sound conservative, fundamental, evangelical theologians from no less than two distinct cultures have struggled with it. I suggest that all theologies should be written jointly to guard against a one culture point of view.

The translator uses the key to the translation process, the functional equivalent. This is called by some the dynamic equivalent or "redemptive analogy" as in the book the Peace Child. Our friends among the Pocomchi Indian people of Guatemala were scandalized to realize that the bodies of Ananias and Sapphira were not bathed before burial. They considered that as heathen and pagan, even as we do the practice of placing the corpse on a raised platform, to be picked at by the vultures, or on a pyre to be consumed by fire. Nowhere is it stated that their bodies were washed, but the translation process that is a responsible one must include somewhere the indication that the burial was a Christian burial, fully and completely accepted by God. This indication may only be a footnote that the body was washed, but it must be there for the Pocomchi.

I stumbled over this principle early in the process of translation for a Maya related people of Central America. I was translating in the book of Luke, chapter 13 where Herod is referred to as a "fox". In Pocomchi, the word for fox is <u>bahlam</u> but upon using the word, I received a very strange reaction. Enquiring further, I discovered that a fox to the Pocomchi is not seen as sly and crafty -- that is what the wildcat is. Rather the fox talks with a falsetto. Once I had clarified the point utilizing the word for wildcat, their reaction to the entire chapter revealed to me that they had grasped the truth intended in the passage. Had I continued with the word "fox" they would have learned falsehood.

The <u>researcher</u>. Persons in every other category must also engage in behavioral research in order to fulfill their function adequately. Research is the foundation upon which the behavioral sciences are built. There is a valid place in mission for the objective research as such, especially in two areas, 1) to study all factors and participants involved in the complex interaction between two or more cultures in contact in mission, 2) to study and evaluate the effectiveness of mission in its varying endeavors. Many missions make use of the techniques of behavioral sciences research as applied to mission as for example through MARC.

The behavioral sciences do not present the Christian and the missionary a panacea. The blessings are mixed and the use of the various disciplines and principles call for discernment. Every thought, every action, every relationship needs to be literally bathed in prayer.

1. We must remember that whatever approach is used in mission there need to be results. If what we learn and practice through the behavioral sciences is ineffectual for conversion and Christian growth, then that part or that whole of our approach must be set aside.

2. It is easy to manipulate people to our own selfish ends. I have had some students who pursued the behavioral sciences for the sake of power they sensed they would have over people. Their reaction was much like Jason in the book of Acts who coveted the power the disciples displayed but not their experience in Christ. We need to remember that our efforts in mission are not to move people to do <u>our</u> will, rather, that the Spirit of God might act in their lives to guide them into the will of God.

3. Training to become a good researcher is not readily available in North American colleges and universities. Courses are offered in very few schools. The training also comes late – after most people have their life styles established. Further the training is minimal in comparison to all the other education

a missionary gets. Finally, it is seen as non-academic, low-status, and relatively unprofitable. As behavioral scientists we must act to improve the academic image of relationship training and research orientation. Also, we need to introduce such training at the high school level at least, if not earlier; in the church, even if it is not yet in the school. Finally, we must design courses and programs that will have the desired effect in preparation of research oriented missionaries who use this as a solid foundation to their mission effort.

The training to be a behavioral researcher needs to be offered where populations are available to be researched. You cannot learn researching by lecture, you must be participating in it to know what it is all about. Thus, the teacher must be an effective researcher. If distinct cultures are not available for research then subcultures need to be studied for the experience. The teacher provides the continuity of research in the subculture.

4. Counseling is not a "telling" interaction. Rather it is an experience of discovery, where the one being counseled begins to discover for himself/herself what has gone sour in the life, what can be done about it. The person is thus given principles and clues, goes out and works on his own life a while, returns and as the debriefing progresses gains new insights which can be taken out and tried and assimilated into the life. Good counseling is not an injection type experience, rather, a carefully guided experience in living.

5. Not all secular theorists are wrong. I think it is easy for us in Christian circles to think that because we have the truth in Jesus Christ, we have the truth in everything and all the truth there is. This is just not so and we need a great deal of humility in treating other theorists and their thoughts. Whatever you may think of Carl Rogers, his "helping relationship" is tremendous and needs to be internalized by every missionary serving Christ anywhere.

6. On the other hand, not all Christians have good behavioral sciences nor sound principles which they are peddling under the guise of Christian and Bible truth. We must be especially diligent in these days to sort out the truth from the falsehood, the useful from the useless.

7. We must have intelligent Christians evaluating our work. This cannot be left to biased, bigoted, narrow, unread, slow to understand reviewers. We must pray that God will raise up a whole host of intelligent, thinking Christians who are learned and discerning.

8.   Translation is the most complex and demanding of all
the challenges to the behavioral scientist. It involves the
Biblical cultures, our own culture, the other's culture who is
to receive the translation. The functional equivalent must be
provided for the whole context as well as for any one part.
Otherwise, a specific message might be received intact but the
total impression of the truth might be lacking, the integration
of the whole. Finally, the translator must have sound doctrine
and teaching, not just in words but in every respect.

9.   To accomplish our purposes in mission we need the full
cooperation of behavioral scientists, theologians, missions
profs and administrators. Mission today is more than ever a
team effort. Cooperation established by the Spirit of God and
carried out by that very same Spirit is the order of the day.

The contributions of behavioral sciences in mission lie in
areas of evangelism and personal spiritual growth of the
missionary as well as the recipient of the "good news".

1.   People in any society and culture will be guided into
the acceptance of Jesus Christ as Savior. They will not find
themselves pressed to embrace just a new culture or lifestyle,
or another cultural way of viewing Christ.

2.   The behavioral sciences will aid in reducing personal
and interpersonal tension. People, as James says, will develop
patience with themselves and with one another. We objectify
our lived experience so we can more fully understand the other,
and more readily control our own behavior in interaction with
the other.

3.   Such training and preparation will aid in reducing the
tensions felt between the missionary and the national.

4.   There is likely to be more positive contribution to
the every day lives of the people among whom we minister.
Christianity can relate more to the felt need of the people as
well as to the real need they share for knowing Jesus Christ.

5.   God will provide the "well done thou good and faithful
servant," and the people, whom we serve, will provide, "we're
glad you've lived among us."

The behavioral sciences as applied in mission are not to
supplant the truth, rather, enhance it; are not to become com-
petitive with theology and sound doctrine, rather aid and cooperate in communicating truth to all men; are not designed to
displace Jesus Christ as Savior and Lord, but rather, to allow

each person in their own cultural setting, to know fully and completely this one who loved us and gave Himself for us.

12
REACHING UNREACHED PEOPLES

by George W. Peters

Our Lord repeated the Great Commission to His disciples at
several occasions. As far as I know, it is the only command
that in one form or another is repeated six times in the gospels
and in the book of Acts. I said to myself, "Well, if the disciples needed the message to be repeated that often, perhaps
the Lord wants to tell us something in a very special way because I, too, will repeat last night's message to some degree."
I am not at all embarrassed because of this. I do feel that
it is an emphasis the Lord wants us to hear. My subject was
assigned to me. It reads: "Reaching the Unreached." And that
is going to be my emphasis. My colleague, Dr. Winter, emphasized the unreached people. I will place my emphasis, therefore,
after a brief review, more upon reaching the unreached. Thus
we will complement each other, I believe, in a wonderful way.
May the Lord speak to us! It seems to me, brethren and sisters,
that the Lord is moving upon us in order to move us out a little
more than we have been venturing out.

My source material for this lecture comes, to some extent,
from personal research. On the other hand, I have greatly benefited by several books, pamphlets, and some articles. I am
greatly indebted to World Vision, first because of its magazine
which usually adds one page devoted to a study of a country.
Perhaps I am the only one, but I have xeroxed all of them in
order to preserve them nicely in files, country by country.
This helps me to keep up to date on what is being published.
Next came the great piece of research work on the profiles of
the countries which provide excellent material. It was published by MARC for the Lausanne Conference.

George W. Peters, consultant to many mission agencies, is Emeritus Chairman of the Department of World Missions at Dallas Theological Seminary and Emeritus Director of the World Missions Research Center. He has had pastoral experience and was once dean
of the Mennonite Biblical Seminary. He holds the B.A. and Ph.D.
degrees, the latter from Hartford Seminary Foundation, and is
author of *Suburban Evangelism* and *A Biblical Theology of Missions*.

I have greatly benefited by the Wycliffe Translators which
have, no doubt, the greatest up-to-date listing of the tribal
peoples of the world. Anyone who is interested to go into that
type of ministry ought to correspond with Wycliffe Translators.
They may send you a list of the 2,000 tongues to go, and you will
find more material than you will be willing to accept or to
follow through. So there is the second source of the Wycliffe
Translators. I am also greatly indebted to Dr. Ed Pentecost
who did much of the research for MARC. He published his book:
Reaching the Unreached. I gladly introduce this piece of work
here to you. If you have not seen it please take note of it.
He prepared it in a special way for the Lausanne Conference on
reaching the unreached. There is a great deal of material in
this book for anyone who is looking for a new mission field
somewhere in the world. You will find here quite some listings.
It is a very good handbook to have.

I have found much material and perhaps the most up-to-date
information in a book that was published in Africa, in Pretoria,
by a certain Mr. Johnston. He has accepted this as his special
mission project and has published a book on "Operation World."
I do not know where you can find a better handbook on country-
by-country listings of the strength of the religious movements,
of Protestantism and evangelicals and the missions operating,
etc., than you will find in this book. It is an excellent handbook and full of information. (It has been reprinted by William
Carey Library.)

The World Dominion Press is being followed to a limited
extent by Worldwide Evangelization Crusade, which has published
some good material. The Challenge of the Unachieved was printed in 1961. The same year they published a book on world survey.
In 1971 they released a very fine booklet, really a mimeograph-
ed pamphlet entitled They Are Bread For Us. It presents very
fine materials on what is being done and what needs to be done.
Then again in 1973 they published a book here which is describ-
ing world awakenings. It, too, is full of information on the
subject we are discussing.

Naturally, I should not forget to mention the tremendous
work that Dr. Ralph Winter has done in this field. He has
given to us a great deal of statistical material, especially
in his charts and other presentations. I have also found wonderful material in government publications. In fact, the most
up-to-date information that I did find on Nigeria in 1968 was
at the University, not with the missions. There are census
reports which clearly tabulate how many Muslims and how many
Christians there were, and then the middle belt of what they
called the pagan world. It was evident from the sources that

Islam had expanded only in proportion to the expansion of the
population. It had made few, if any, new converts from the pagan
population. I have searched high and low in Nigeria, Western
Africa, and in Eastern Africa, to find documentation for the
statements that were noised abroad years ago that for every
Christian that was being made five or six people were being converted to Islam. We have searched for documentation but did not
find any kind of verification. So we finally dismissed it as
somebody's guess. In government documents we found the statistics that Islam had grown only as fast as the population had
expanded. However, the Christian population had expanded not
only as fast as their population had increased, but had won
converts from the non-Christians to the degree that these have
not increased in some thirty-five or forty years. They still
constitute the same belt. Later Gerald Swank caught the vision,
and SIM and ECWA are doing a noble work in invading the neglected
areas. They are setting an example in all-out evangelism. We
need to follow them in country after country.

Another very helpful source of information came to me some
years ago when I was in Colombia. Again, it was at the anthropological museum and in the government's Department of Education
where I found the most up-to-date statistics on all the different religious movements. The same thing held true in Indonesia:
the government had the statistics. Again, I have a handbook on
India on the tribal people of that land. The government gives
all the information on over 300 tribal people in India, their
geographical location, their numbers and what is being done for
them, either culturally, socially, or in every other way.

Thus anyone who wants information on the unreached peoples
does not need to remain in ignorance. There is considerable information on the unreached peoples of the world.

Now then, what does this reveal to me? It reveals that we
have in the world _major blocs_ either geographically or as people
that must be classified as practically unreached people. You
may be surprised when I begin, first of all, with _Europe_. Oh
yes, I do believe that Europe to a great extent, is an unevangelized continent. No European will take offense in this. I
understand my European friends well that they do not like to be
classified as a mission field. They certainly recognize several
countries as tremendously needy areas of evangelism. They welcome evangelists. Though they do not appreciate the word
missions, they do appreciate the word evangelism. We need to
consider seriously the large northern belt of the _Mediterranean_.
Here we have Spain, Italy, Albania, Yugoslavia, Greece, and
Rumania. Here is a bloc of people in desperate need of the
gospel. Except Albania all others can be reached in one way or

another, some more freely, some more limited. We have here a
bloc of approximately 140,000,000 people who constitute one of
the most needy and most unreached people of the world.

We have relatively few missionaries in these countries.
There are far more missionaries per capita in Latin America or
in Africa or in Japan or in Indonesia than there are in these
sections of the world. There they are--completely destitute of
the gospel of Jesus Christ. And yet one of the most open fields
as far as governments are concerned. They are open to us and
they are open to the gospel of Jesus Christ. I consider Italy
one of the most open fields to the gospel that we have in all of
Europe. There is the tremendous bloc of the north rim of the
Mediterranean.

The second great bloc was mentioned to us yesterday. It
is the Muslim world. The Muslim world is a stark reality. We
usually speak of 500,000,000. I personally have my questions
here because I cannot very well classify Indonesia as a Muslim
country though there are millions of Muslims there. Indonesia
is only superficially and not really Islamic. Only thirty-five
percent, thirty-seven at the most, have ever registered themselves as Muslims. All the rest of them, if anything, are only
statistically Muslims. Be that as it is, the Muslim world is a
tremendous bloc. We should not consider them as closed. There
are areas that we can enter. Iran is one of the most open fields
today in the Muslim world, besides, or course, Indonesia, as I
mentioned already.

The third bloc was also mentioned yesterday. It is what
we call the caste people of India, 500,000,000 of them at least.
These are the true Hindus. Somehow we have bypassed the Muslim
and the caste people to a great extent simply because there were
so many of the harijans that responded to the gospel.

It needs to be established that the caste people are not
responding to the gospel. We cannot speak with absoluteness
nor do I believe anyone can. However, according to the best of
studies, we have only a very small percentage of caste people
that have come into the church of India. The vast majority of
the members come either from the harijans (the outcasts, the
untouchables), or from tribal people. In the last years more
are coming from the caste people. The amazing thing is the
openness of the present.

We spent some time in India. In fact, I was helping one
of the men there with some research work along the line of
caste evangelism. He is gathering material on first generation
converts from the Brahmin and higher caste people. In three

months that he was there, he gathered up information on considerable numbers of people. Tremendous things are going on
among the caste people of India today. No one can persuade me
anymore that the caste people of India are closed to the gospel
of Jesus Christ. However, they have remained unreached to a
great extent. Perhaps they are as much neglected as they are
unreachable.

China is closed to missionaries, not necessarily to the
gospel. Radio penetrates every area of the world. Some 800
million people are walled off from the rest of the world but
not necessarily from God.

There is the fourth world, the world of tribal people to
which I have referred already. However, one of the greatest
challenges before us comes to us from the concrete jungles of
the Third World cities. Perhaps you realize that of the twenty-
five largest and fastest growing cities of the world, twelve are
located in Asia. Only three are in the United States. Only
four of them are in Latin America, only five in Europe (including London), only one in Africa, but twelve are in Asia. The
vast concrete jungles of the cities of the Orient will soon
constitute a world by themselves. For me, they become one of
the greatest challenges that missions is facing in our generation. I say a hearty "amen" to some of the things that were
said here this morning when it was emphasized that, "We ought
to go to the areas where the life pulse is beating, and evangelize there." This means the cities of Asia.

I find very few of the mission societies who are really
specializing in city evangelism in the foreign countries. Yet
this is one of the crying needs. I hope that God in some way
can speak to us about reaching into these multi-million cities
and that we in some way can penetrate them with the gospel of
Jesus Christ.

These are some of the masses that are before us and some
major blocs of unreached people referred to yesterday.

You see then some of the major blocs that must have the
gospel. Only spiritual blindness and cold indifference to the
eternal welfare of people can speak of missionary moratorium.
We need all the manpower we can mobilize to get the job done.

My major emphasis this evening is on reaching the unreached. What can we do to reach these unreached peoples? I
do not expect to say many new things to you, except outline
here in eight or nine points what I feel we ought to be thinking about. Number one, we must place ourselves under the orders

of God, fully convinced that God wants these people to be reached. There is no question in my mind, my brethren and sisters, that God wants those people to be reached with the gospel of Jesus Christ. I cannot accept the theory, no matter how strong a Calvinist I am trying to be, I cannot console myself with the idea that God has predestinated them simply to remain without the gospel. I find this to be in clearest contradiction to anything that my Bible teaches. It is not the will of God that they should perish, and if God so loved the world that He gave His only begotten Son for them, He certainly means for you and me to love them to the degree that we bring them the good news of Jesus Christ. God wants them to be reached.

The second point that I am making is this: We must set out with a deep faith, that they are reachable and winable. I have given a great deal of thought to this very point. It is not so easy for me to make this statement simply because I, too, wrestle continuously with different philosophies, different approaches and different theories, etc. It is more scriptural to believe that they are reachable, that they are winable, than to speak of testing the soil. Human standards are too mis-leading to be determined by them. This leads us to the question: Why? Why are we not reaching them?

Last winter I was teaching a short winter course in Virginia. I was teaching a course in evangelism. At that occasion I took my class to Lynchburg, to Jerry Falwell's church. I had written him and made an appointment requesting an interview. We wanted to learn some lessons from him. After all, it is a church that has succeeded in winning at least between twenty and twenty-five percent of the city into one church. In our conversation I posed this question: "Tell me, how do you go about reaching these people with the gospel?" Upon this he made a statement which for me was classic. Said he: "From the very beginning we prayed and prayed that God would give us the conviction, the solid, absolute conviction that every man is reachable with the gospel if we only find the key to his heart." Then he added: "God has not let us down."

I know you might ask me where does that leave you with the theory so prevalent today of going to the areas of high potential. I must admit that this is not my problem. I am much more concerned in obeying the Lord than following some theories. I am not here to discount this or that, but my emphasis is to reach the unreached whoever they may be. It is my deep conviction that God has His people among the Muslims. He has His people among the caste people of India. He has them among the hardened Europeans. He has them in the Catholic belt and Greek Orthodox communities. It is for you and for me

to go and find the way to the hearts of these people and to win
them to the Lord Jesus Christ, claim them by simple faith, and
in fervent prayer, until we break through whatever the barriers
may be. We must win them to the Lord. That is my command from
the Lord, and I cannot help but stand on it. And I do believe
that if He commands me to do it, there is a possibility of
doing it. I am searching for methods, for ways of communicating.
I am searching for a key to the hearts of these people. I will
come more fully upon it later when I speak of the relevant
message.

But here we must set ourselves in firm faith, believing
that they can be reached, they are winable. By the grace of
God we will win them.

My third point of emphasis relates to prayer. This is
something that comes very close to me. I was deeply, deeply
touched by this very truth that I want to emphasize here.

The spring before last, I had the privilege of being at
Mount Hermon for a week's conference. We thought we had a
wonderful conference. At the close of the very last day, a
lady came to me, an elderly lady, a godly woman, at least that
is what the people told me. She said, "Brother Peters, I have
been listening now for a whole week here." It so happened that
Leighton Ford was there and myself, as the two speakers. She
said, "I have enjoyed every session, every one of them. But
how come, we have been talking for the whole week about missions
and we have not had a single day of prayer for missions?"

Then she made a statement that is something for you and for
me to ponder. She said, "I think back twenty-five, forty years
ago the many invitations we had for mission prayer conferences.
How come we do not have those conferences now anymore?"

My brethren and sisters, I could not help but go away from
there deeply depressed. I do not want to be overcritical, but
I have been watching it pretty closely. We have become in
missions so wrapped up in technology and methodology that we
have forgotten that missions is number one the releasing of
divine dynamics. This brings me to my point: reaching the
unreached will, first of all, mean for us, not only to lay
hold of it in faith, but to develop thousands and thousands of
prayer cells in America and elsewhere that will commit themselves wholeheartedly to prayer until the victory will be won.
My dear people, I do believe God will bring us to our knees
as never before as we will face some of the issues in missions.
It is my deep conviction that reaching the unreached will have
to be done, number one, on our knees. Our knees and our churches

our knees and our constituency. I was discussing a ministry with
one of the executives. It is a ministry that could involve me
personally. We are continuously in need of finances and are
burdened with many cares. I have no answers for many of these
matters. Our greatest need, however, is the releasing of divine
power that will smite the enemy and conquer the foe. We need
spiritual mobilization. After six months in the Orient this
year, I am deeply convinced that technology and methodology, as
good as they are, will never win the battle. It will be won
either in the power of God in response to prayer, or we will
keep on chopping away, but the tree will not come down.

So here is my third point: mobilizing thousands of people
in specific prayer for specific areas, for specific fields.
This is what we must do.

Number four, and this may sound almost like a contradiction,
but it is not. It is a complement, supplement, if you want to.
We must discover strategic bridges for the gospel into these
areas. Just a few days ago I was reading something on Kuwait.
Most of us know little about Kuwait, and those who know just
write it off as a country that gives us all kinds of pain in our
neck because of the oil struggles. On the other hand, we hardly
realize that Kuwait may be our very best bridge into the Arabic
world. Kuwait has thus far stood firmly, resolutely for total
religious freedom. On the other hand, sixty-five percent of all
the population of Kuwait are immigrants from other countries
that are open to the gospel.

Could Kuwait become our bridgehead into the Arabic world?
Could God keep this open in some way or open a wedge and a door
for us to enter in with the gospel of Jesus Christ? I have
already mentioned Iran. We spent some time in Iran. I had
been there before. The present reports are much more encouraging. A much freer air seems to flow and the missionaries seem
to move about with the gospel of Jesus Christ much more freely.
They felt perfectly free, perfectly safe, as though the whole
country was gradually, gradually opening up for the gospel of
Jesus Christ.

Iran may not be a bridge into the Arabic world because of
the tension and the Iranians being a different people. But it
could be a bridge into the Turkish world. It could be a bridge
into Afghanistan. It could be a bridge into Pakistan much
more than it has been thus far. It is this kind of studies that
we must carry on in order to find the different bridges that we
can best occupy in order to proceed into the unreached areas and
to the people.

Let me go to <u>point five</u> in my suggestions. We need to
engage in careful, comprehensive, and in-depth research to locate the unreached people, first of all. I have here two overhead transparencies, one on Italy and one on Spain. For instance, here you have the information on Spain (a map). Here
you can locate the areas that are not occupied. Barcelona
has quite a number of churches. You have quite a number of
churches in Madrid. Of course, these are relatively few when
you think of the large population. Madrid is one of the twenty-
five largest cities in the world. But here we see the type of
research that needs to be done. I wish I could challenge us
here to carry through this type of research in country after
country so that we would have the information.

I have here a similar chart on Italy. If you want to know
how far Italy is occupied, how far it is evangelized, look at
this. Total provinces are without a single Christian Protestant
witness. This is why we say that we have here some of the most
unoccupied fields. By the way, all of Italy, 55,000,000 people
have about 250 missionaries. Allowing for furlough time, we
have between 175 and 200 missionaries steadily in the work
there. Thank God, we have churches here as you see.

This map on Italy was drawn by a Roman Catholic priest.
He did it for the Vatican in order to inform them how the
Protestants were progressing in Italy. They were kind enough
to let us have the information. So we thanked them for the fine
research work they have been doing for us.

A fine and informative map on Japan is available. It
shows exactly how far the different areas in the country are
evangelized, what has been done, what must be done. It is my
contention that evangelical forces ought to rally together and
in some way produce similar maps on field after field, that
we would have exactly before us how far we have gone in each
country. This is the information that we need.

Having done careful research and having found the unreached
people, we continue our research. Here I follow the late Dr.
J.H. Bavinck of Holland who says that in any country, any culture, any people, any religion, we will find that no matter how
strongly the people try to envelop themselves in their culture
and religion, God in His wonderful, marvelous grace keeps a
crack somewhere in order to wedge in the gospel of Jesus Christ.
And it is for us to go into these areas, to search out diligently and find out exactly where that crack is. This is what we
are doing with the Brahmins in a research project.

We have now a considerable number of testimonies written out. Many of them are in Hindi, and others in Tamil, etc. I cannot read them. But they will be made available to us. We are searching for answers to two questions: (1) What were your basic difficulties in becoming a Christian? What was in your way, and (2) What was it in the gospel that helped you overcome those difficulties? From the answers evolves quite a wonderful pattern. If we can define the problems we can find a message that will help them to overcome the difficulties. This is what we need to know. This is what we need to study carefully in order to wedge our way in to reach the unreached. Dr. Perez spoke to us this morning on identification. It is my deep conviction, my brethren and sisters, that if we want to communicate with these people in a manner that is meaningful to them, it will take a deep, deep identification with them. At the same time we will have to communicate to them in a manner that is relevant to them.

This brings me to <u>point six:</u> each area and people will demand a specific type of strategy, unique method, unique emphasis and message in sowing and in reaping. We speak today glowingly and to the glory of God of the tremendous response to the gospel in Latin America. But brethren and sisters, let's never forget that no continent has had more suffering colporteurs than Latin America has had. They together with the radio have unlocked the continent. We speak of the tremendous openings in Africa. Do not forget that no continent has buried more missionaries as Africa has. There is a reason for the abundance of the harvest. In Latin America it has come one way. In Africa it has come another way. In Japan it is yet another way. I see no other way to reach Japan than television. You say it is expensive. I know it is, and we will need to make the decision either to reach them by television and pay for it or not reach them at all.

I shall never forget the challenge that came to us when we were there for the conference on communication. A Shinto gentleman stood before us and gave us one of the best lectures on television. Finally in his last five minutes he gave me the biggest mission challenge that I have ever had. As a Shinto he looked at us and said, "You Christians. You claim to have a message which all men should hear."

I said to myself, "Well, he got something."

"When," he said, "will you wake up and make it possible for them to hear?' We looked at him. "Gentlemen and ladies," he said, "Japan will hear you if you will give it to them on television."

Naturally, when he was through, a group of us was right around him. A lengthy conversation resulted which stimulated and motivated all of us. The question still remains: when will we make the gospel available to Japan in an appealing manner?

Number seven. We must carefully prepare men and women to pioneer such specific assignments. I make no apology here. I would like to see mature, experienced missionaries transfer from their well-established work into unreached areas. Relocation of missionaries is not easy but it is essential. Tomorrow I want to speak on strategic withdrawal of missionaries and relocating missionaries. This is one of the points which needs much prayerful consideration. Missionaries of experience ought to be placed into pioneer ministries especially among people where going is difficult.

The eighth point is a rather perplexing suggestion. We need to design united programs of several missions in order to develop strong and relevant ministries to specific areas and/or people. This is something we have not majored on, except that a wonderful program is going on in Nepal where a number of missionaries are cooperating. It seems to me that if we really want to reach the unreached, we will have to go into team ministries. Really this should not be so difficult.

Practically all of us subscribe to the same doctrinal statement. We draw missionaries from the same schools, get our finances and prayer support from the same churches. Why shouldn't we build teams of different missions and work together when absolutely necessary or more advantageous?

I come to the last point. We need to prayerfully consider assistance to churches and missions in the Third World and help them develop their missionary resources. They need and desire to advance in evangelism and missions beyond their present abilities and possibilities and/or in the areas and to people who are not open to Western missionaries. I make no apology for making such a statement. If we want to reach the unreached, there are areas where we will have to develop stronger team ministries with brethren and sisters of the Third World. The church of Jesus Christ is not lacking in resources. I spent ten weeks in Korea, lectured in four different seminaries. What a thrill to have 600 young people before you in a seminary chapel. I tell you it means something. We had special sessions in missions. The basic question was: how can we get out? A gentleman told me, "Don't challenge them too much. We cannot send so many."

Why? He said, "The churches are not prepared, nor do we
have the finances to send them out." I question it on the one
hand. On the other hand, I know that there are countries that
cannot do it.

I challenge you openly and publicly to think seriously on
this matter. There is manpower in this world that can be tapped.
Can we find a basis on which we can operate together? On the
other hand, there are areas in which we are not welcome. On
the other hand, are we willing to help them that they can move
into areas where they are welcome and they are willing to do the
work?

These are some of the things that burden my heart in
reaching the unreached. Let me conclude with this statement.
Brethren and sisters, I do believe God is a just God. He has
not placed us under a burden that we cannot handle. If He has
commanded us that the gospel is to be preached to every creature,
it can be done. He is not that type of taskmaster who places
us before a responsibility that we cannot handle. He is too
just to do that. It is for you and for me to place ourselves,
number one, under the command of Him who issued the Great
Commission. It is for you and for me, then, on our knees to
advance and to search for ways and means that it can be done.
I am convinced that we have all the means at our disposal today
to make the gospel available in one form or another and to make
the gospel available to every creature. We must accept the
challenge to reach the unreached.

13

ISSUES CONFRONTING EVANGELICAL MISSIONS

by George W. Peters

Permit me to thank the brethren for inviting me to come here and share some of the burdens that are gathering upon our hearts as we travel, as we study, as we work.

Last night I shared with you the burden of reaching the unreached. Today it is a message of a different nature. I am sorry I do not have it written out. In fact, I was informed that it was not necessary. It would be taped. Then we hope to edit it somewhat, and you can read it later. So be of good cheer and please listen attentively.

It may also be that if you listen attentively, you need not read it later. Take your choice and see what we get on with. Let me say that I appreciate being here. It has been my privilege to attend these meetings for a number of years. I can honestly say that they have been very enriching to me. I get aspects of missions here that I do not get on the battlefield or in the classroom. So we appreciate the balance that comes into our work in this manner. We thank God for the fellowship, as well as for the ministries which you are rendering. I will need to leave this afternoon but I want to wish you the Lord's richest blessings. Please, remember one thing, even if you forget everything else: 'God wants this world to be reached with the gospel!' And if He wants it, it can be done! There is however one statement of our Lord that has puzzled me a great deal. One of the writers reports that He could do there no mighty work. What? He could not? No, He could do there no mighty work. The reason is because of their unbelief. That is

George W. Peters, consultant to many mission agencies, is Emeritus Chairman of the Department of World Missions at Dallas Theological Seminary and Emeritus Director of the World Mission Research Center. He has had pastoral experience and was once dean of the Mennonite Biblical Seminary. He holds the B.A. and Ph.D. degrees, the latter from Hartford Seminary Foundation, and is author of *Suburban Evangelism* and *A Biblical Theology of Missions*.

the only limitation you and I can cast upon the omnipotence of
God. May God be gracious to us as a church of Jesus Christ that
we will not limit Him!

I shall never forget a statement a professor of mine made
when we were studying Romans. The question was raised, "Professor, what will God do with those who are dying in ignorance?"

The professor's answer was, "I know God is just. God is
loving, but also that He is holy and righteous. He will have
His way of dealing with those people."

My question is not primarily what God will do with the
unbelieving people that are dying in ignorance, my concern is,
what will He do with the church that leaves them in such ignorance? That is also my burning question. What will He do with
the mission societies that are not moving, that have homesteaded
instead of being a mission sent? What will He do with the
churches that are not moving, that are not sending and then are
not making the light available?

This morning we are facing a different issue. The subject
is: Issues confronting evangelical missions! I must deal with
it from an entirely different point of view than the one we
discussed yesterday. This burden is not much less heavy on my
heart than the previous one. We must learn to think with God
about the deep issues of the gospel. The situation is complex
and we are in danger to so generalize the issues that our discussion could become an empty thing. Let us keep in mind that
what I am bringing to you this morning has been gathered from
all the different continents. It has been rolling upon us from
time to time and gathered up here and there. Specific issues
relate to specific fields and you will have to ask yourselves:
does this relate to my field, to our ministry?

One of the great sins that missiology has committed, is
the sin of creating a world image of missions. There is no
world image of missions. There is an image of missions for
every particular country and people. I found this one of the
most frustrating things for the missionaries in Japan. I
learned this after I had been there a number of times before.
This time I came there after nine weeks of having been saturated
in Korea where everything is just tumbling, so to speak, just
moving in a tremendous way. It is easy to project the Korean
mission image over Japan, but this is unscientific, unfair, un-
realistic.

I started to use illustrations from Korea in Japan but I
quickly stopped it. That was not the mission world of Japan,

and has caused endless frustrations in the hearts of the people.
So I carefully selected my illustrations from areas of Japan.
There are things happening in Japan. I had to do the same
thing when we came to the Philippines. There is an image of
missions of the Philippines, I hope that God keeps me from con-
fusing and frustrating people. Each country and people has its
own images. This also relates to issues. I could create for
you an image of issues that will become, so to speak, a blanket
covering the whole world. But this would not be a true image.
There are some issues in Africa that relate peculiarly to
Africa. There are some issues in Latin America. There are some
issues in Asia, some in Europe, and even some in the United
States. These are facts we must keep in mind. I hope we can
sort out and learn this in our studies.

Now let us turn to the issues as they have come to us. I
want to divide them basically into two greater sections:
1. The issues as they relate to the administrative operational
level and 2. Issues as they relate to the theological level.

What are some of the issues that evangelical missions must
face, continue to face on the administrative operational levels?
Number one is still the issue of the church-missions relationship.

It is instructive to observe how this moves from country
to country and from place to place. Twelve years ago we spent
quite a time in Japan. I was teaching there in a seminary
and moved about quite extensively. Not one comment did I hear
at that time on the church-missions relationships. Seemingly
things were going so beautifully and so smoothly. I had just
come from India. Here church-missions relationship was a very
hot issue. The year before I had been in Africa. Here, too
it was a much discussed issue. In Japan everything was quiet.
Things have changed drastically. This time we spent six weeks
in Japan with five different missions. In every one of them
this has become a crucial issue.

Somehow this moves about and comes to a climax in country
by country. No, Green Lake did not solve the problem of the
church-missions relationships. We hope it did give some direction, it pointed some ways. But the issue is not resolved
in a number of countries. I did not sense it this time in India.
I sensed it in two missions in Korea. The rest of them somehow
had been able to regulate it. It is still a very crucial issue
in a number of areas. I want to challenge in a special way the
missions in Latin America. This is one of the most crucial
questions at the present in Latin America. How can we relate
the church and the missions?

I have no solutions at the present to offer, because I am speaking here on issues that you are to discuss later and find the answers. I merely draw your attention to it. Green Lake has pointed ways, given directions, and it has helped solve the issue in many fields with a number of missions. My burden is because of those missions who seemingly try to bypass the issues and are becoming a negative reflection on all the evangelical missions. This is something that ought to be placed upon the heart and conscience of every evangelical mission leader. Remember, that in the mission field you are not the only mission. Whatever happens to your mission in one way or another is picked up by spokesmen for the people and often used against missions in general. It is generalized in such a way that it reflects negatively upon the total evangelical cause. This we ought to take very, very seriously.

The second issue is the matter of financial aid or assistance to the younger churches. It is my impression that we have made this into a problem. It seems to me quite legitimate that we should render them financial help. It is possible to be of assistance to the younger churches without being paternalistic. I do believe that we owe them more than manpower or wisdom or history, etc. We do have an obligation to our sister churches because God has so richly and so bountifully blessed us. Admittedly, this is one of the precarious matters: how can we do this without permitting to arise within ourselves a feeling of benevolence, without creating within ourselves the feeling of paternalism, consciously or unconsciously? At the same time, how can we do this so that the recipient will not feel an over-indebtedness to us and become bound and his freedom become limited? Or that he develops a feeling of dependence upon us? Or that our assistance becomes a stifling factor in their sense of sacrifice and their sense of responsibility.

To regulate our financial assistance to the churches in the Third World demands a great deal of humility, wisdom and the presence of the Holy Spirit in all of us. This is an area we need to deal with in the presence of God and in a manner that the Holy Spirit can lead both sides, the donor and recipient. They must come to an understanding of brotherliness that is not in any way influenced by finances. I do believe that it can be accomplished by the ministry of the Holy Spirit.

This leads me to the third issue on the administrative operational level. It too relates to finances. It is the support of national ministries that are not directly and exclusively related to our mission and church. A concrete illustration is a joint seminary. I have been very happy to read what

is being done by a number of missions about the Yeotmal Seminary.
I believe they are right in trying to relocate. It is just as
evident that they cannot do this alone.

Here is a mission, a project which renders a vital ministry.
How will it be done? How free, how liberal will we be in the
support of a project from which the nation and the evangelical
church as a whole gain far more than my own mission will? Here
we need special grace in our ministry and the administration of
the Lord's finances. I plead again and I make no apology for
another movement. I believe in it wholeheartedly and more so
after this ministry of six months in the Orient. I am referring
to the World Evangelical Fellowship. I am not saying that this
is a movement that has no faults. If it did, it would belong to
New Jerusalem and not into our times. It so happens that it
has its faults, its limitations. Yet, my brethren and sisters,
I am deeply convinced that we need an association that in some
way binds together the total evangelical movement around the
world. We need it in Africa. We need it in Asia. We need it
in Europe. We need it here. We need it in Latin America. Unless we will be bound together, we will find ourselves depleted
in our ranks one by one by forces that are not welcome to us.
The question is: how free, how solidly will we stand behind
such movements in which I personally, and my mission may not be
gaining very much. This is the question our national brethren
are raising again and again, an issue we need to deal with in
the Spirit of God.

From this I change to my next subject which needs depth-
research and discussion. I am referring to the life-style and
operational budget of the American missionaries. This is a very
crucial and critical matter. It is a fact that the American
missionary in most countries lives on an economic level so far
above everyone else that he seems like a millionaire to many
people. We heard yesterday a message on identification. I said
to myself, "Yes, he is touching upon a very, very sensitive
spot." Identification cuts deep into our life and life-style.

Comparing the American missionary to the European and the
British missionaries and some of the others, it is evident that
we are economically out of proportion. It cannot be established,
however, that our effectiveness is so much greater. It creates
a distance in the missionary family that you sense very deeply
once you get close into the fellowship of others. This has
created in me a rather sensitive conscience. You know that my
cradle stood in Europe. Now I am enjoying the plenty and the
bounty of America. However, I cannot help but feel deeply for
the total movement around the world. I like to see the evangelical forces move together as a solid brotherhood, as a company

of committed men of God who stand shoulder-to-shoulder, as one
army moving ahead. Yet, it is a solemn fact that the economic
level of the American missionaries creates boundaries if not
barriers which are not too pleasant.

On the other hand, this brings with it difficulties if we
want to think in terms of international teams. Without a question that becomes one of the greatest needs in the evangelistic
thrust in many of the larger cities. The international teams
will call for a team mentality that will bring to us serious
problems in the realm of economics. How will we learn to handle
this situation? How will the American learn to stand beside a
brother from India, beside a brother from the Philippines,
beside a brother from Indonesia, from Africa and spend with him
months in a team ministry? These are some serious questions for
us to ponder. At this moment it seems most difficult unless
something happens in our own hearts and minds.

Let us come to the next point which is another serious
issue. I am referring to strategic withdrawal and relocation
of missionaries. Such withdrawal and relocation may serve a
twofold purpose, first to give the national church the possibilities to develop itself, to establish its own identity. And
second, we need to relocate missionaries in order to reach the
unreached. It cannot be established that the numerical
strength of the mission force in a mission field enhances the
growth of the church. No, the growth of the church is not proportional to the number of missionaries that are on a given
field. In fact, some of the smaller missions seemingly have
much more rapid expansion of the Christian church than those
that are well supplied with American personnel. This we need
to emphasize. I realize that this is a question that can be
debated, rationalized, justified as well as explained away.
It is and will remain a perennial problem or issue. However,
a mission that has operated a mission station in an area for
some twenty-five to thirty years, should seriously study its
field and its situation, whether the time has not come to remove its missionaries and relocate them into other areas, perhaps first fifty percent, then eventually seventy-five percent.
Relocation is not demotion. I spoke last night of reaching
the unreached. My brethren, I do not want to be pessimistic.
No, my faith in the sovereignty of God does not permit me to
be pessimistic. On the other hand, I have no reason to believe
that we will greatly expand our mission force from America. If
the unreached are to be reached, we will have to seriously consider relocating missionaries. And missions that have been in
the field twenty-five or thirty-five years should give serious
consideration to begin a gradual, progressive relocation of
missionaries into new areas. Had the Apostle Paul followed the

strategy that many missions were practicing, he would have never moved beyond the Province of Galatia. He could have said, "Here is enough work for me to do. This is where I am." Somehow he had a different strategy. He planted churches in some of the major centers, then he left it to the church to do the evangelizing. He moved on. Somehow we have homesteaded in many areas. We have ceased to be a mission. This is something that we need to reconsider very urgently. The relocation of missionaries, the strategic withdrawal of missionaries is not considered seriously enough.

I hasten to another point on the level of operations which I hope will not be misinterpreted in any way. I throw this out as something we ought to be aware of and be cautious about. There is a danger of polarization of evangelical missions, missionaries, and churches. Because of diverging strategies and methodologies, especially as it relates to the concept of church growth we can divide our forces. It is evident that there are a number of theories of church growth, and each school is quite zealous to propagate its own theories of church growth. Somehow each one has followers. Here is something that I hope we can handle on the home base first, and then carry it into the fields. We need a united front. We cannot afford polarization and a divisive spirit in the mission field. Here we need special grace and wisdom.

From the administrative, operational issues I turn to the theological issues. Theological issues are confronting us and they are coming upon us in full force. The first issue that meets us again and again is the concept of evangelism. We had hoped that Lausanne and the covenant of Lausanne would clarify this issue. It has done so on paper but not in the minds. I have had more questions in India, Japan and in the Philippines about evangelism than I have ever had before. What really is evangelism? In every one of the seminars in India, one of the very first requests was: Define for us evangelism. What do you really mean by evangelism? So we had to go into the nature of what evangelism really means. Somehow evangelicals are not quite sure what evangelism really is. How far does it reach into the area of Christian discipleship-making and of Christian discipleship? How far does it reach into Christianization? How far does it reach into the whole area of radical discipleship, and into social action etc.? Can evangelism be differentiated, if not disassociated from social action? These are questions that are coming up in the seminars that we are conducting in relationship to evangelism. Do not misunderstand. All of these seminars were conducted with evangelical IFMA or EFMA related ministries. Yet, the concept is becoming vague

or hazy and foggy. Schools and missions need to take note of
this. We dare not presuppose many things. We need to be very
careful to clearly define evangelism.

The second issue in relationship to theology is <u>the concept</u>
<u>of the church</u>. In the total realm of operation and function of
missions here is perhaps the most hazy and undefined idea.   I
drew your attention some years ago that somehow the average
American missionary has a low and limited view of the church.
They believe in and speak of church growth. The problem is that
we do not know what a church is. Therefore, how can we make it
grow? We believe in church multiplication, only we do not know
what that church is that is to be multiplied. Is any group of
believers in association a church? The hazy concept of the
church has really troubled me this time more than ever before.
Here is something for the seminary and Bible colleges to work
on. Our people in the fields are not clear on evangelism. They
are not clear on the concept of the church. Where do we stand?
Who has to take the blame? Well, I must say that I place the
blame, number one, into our schools, and secondly into the
orientation programs when the candidates are before you. Somehow we have such a low and hazy view of the church that it
makes us ineffective in church planting. The same vagueness
persists in the minds of the national pastors. I could give
many illustrations. We have sat with groups of missionaries in
Japan, and also groups of the national pastors discussing the
concept of the church. I very quickly discovered that one of the
basic issues why there was tension was because of the divergent
concept of the church. The missionaries had one concept, the
national brother had another concept. It so happened that I had
a third one. I could not accept either one of them. And I am
not so sure whether I sold them on mine or not. You see, after
all, I am an anabaptist who strongly believes in the local
church. I make no hesitation of telling the people that I am a
church man, and I am a denominational man. I am a Mennonite
Brethren, if you want to know. Do not let that scare you. They
are a good people. They are, in fact, conscientious objectors.
They do not trouble anybody, at times not even the unsaved.

Here is one of our fundamental problems. How are our
brethren and sisters in the fields to operate soundly, build a
church, leave a church behind, hand the church over to the
national pastors when they have only a vague concept of what the
church really is? The issue is so pressing that for three
missions in Japan we urged and recommended with all the urgings
within us that next year's annual conference be spent in an in-
tensive study of the concept of the church. We need to come to
grips with this basic issue. Here we are working, working, working, working, for what? Where is our abiding fruit? It has

struck me so deeply. Our Lord says in John 15, that we are to
bring forth fruit, more fruit, much fruit. But then toward the
end He speaks of abiding fruit. The abiding fruit of a mission
in the field is a responsible church. This is our abiding
fruit. However, how can we have abiding fruit when we do not
know what the fruit is? Here is a crucial issue that we have
to work on, clarify it and bring it before the missionaries.
They need and they want our help.

The third issue that I mention is a complicated one. It
is the indigenization and the nationalization of the gospel and
the church. The indigenization and the nationalization or
acculturation of Christianity in the mission field is of para-
mount importance. In some ways this reaches deepest into theology. It leads us into the old question of the relationship
of the church to culture. This is not a simple matter. Saints
and theologians have wrestled with this through the centuries.
There are not ready-made answers. Let no one think that he has
an immediate and a full answer to this question. Anyone who has
any questions along that line ought to read Niebuhr's book on
Christ and Culture. I am not endorsing Niebuhr's theology,
but he has given us from the historical perspective a book which
every missionary ought to read. He brings out what has happened
in the history of Christianity and where one theory has been
tried and another one, and another one, and another one. Seemingly no one has the complete and satisfactory answer to it. I
have been driven into a study of this situation from a different
point of view. Let me say that this is the basic problem of the
church at Corinth. In our studies of cultural anthropology we
make the students go into a comprehensive study of the book of
Corinthians. He is required to list the issues, or the problems
in the church, and then go into the culture of the times. You
will find that every one of the issues that 1 and 2 Corinthians
deal with roots in the culture of the times. We have here a
classical example of "The Gospel and the Church in a Pagan
World." We also have here safe guidelines.

What had happened? The church in Corinth has overaccultura-
ted itself. It had not drawn out its roots deep enough out of
the culture and placed it into Christ and His "Way of Life."
This is a very delicate situation. If you go into one extreme
you are creating a foreign church. This is one of the basic
problems that we need to deal with in Japan. We are dealing
there with the church that is a "Stranger in the Land." Japan
has often been written off as a gospel-hardened resistant
people. This is not true. We have approximately as many professing Christians in Japan as we have in Korea. Three studies
have been carried through; one by the government in its census,
one by the Roman Catholic church, one by a group of Protestants.

They all come up with the same fact that there are in Japan
between three and four million professing Christians. Yet,
when we lump all memberships together, the Roman Catholics,
Greek Orthodox, and Protestants, we have less than a million
members in the churches. Seemingly three million remain outside
of the church. What is the problem? They seemingly have responded to the Gospel at least to Christendom but they do not
respond to the church. That raises the question: Is Robert Lee
accurate when he describes the church, not the gospel, but the
church as "The Stranger in the Land?" This book is one of the
finest case studies that we have on the church in Japan. Is the
trouble in the Church? Is it too divorced from the culture that
the Japanese feels he would be a stranger there? Is this the
problem? Have we created a foreign church? Or is it in the
psychology and the culture of the people? Where seems to be the
difficulty? There seems to be an openness to the gospel. In
fact, it might surprise you that when a comprehensive study was
made in some of the large housing areas in Osaka it was found
that only some twenty percent of the homes had a family shrine.
But a Bible was found in sixty percent of the homes. There
seems to be an openness to the gospel but not to the church.
Is the church irrelevant? Is it too far removed? Where does
the problem lie? We have no answers at the present, but this is
a question that we need to raise. In fact, this is one of the
most serious things that our brethren in Latin America are
wrestling with. This is one of the things the African brethren
are wrestling with.

    There are dangers from both sides. I cannot go into it now,
but certainly there are dangers from both sides. The deepest
problem, however, is not the relationship of the church to its
culture. The deeper problem is on the theological level, and
that is <u>the relevance of the gospel</u>. Is the gospel relevant to
the people to whom we are preaching? One of the Brahmins, an
educated man of India comes out against Christendom in a most
radical way. No, not against Christianity, but against the
Christian church of India. He is a student of the New Testament.
Though he is a red-blooded Brahmin, he reads the New Testament
and studies it thoroughly. He knows it well. He also knows
the sacred writings of Hinduism. He comes to us with a challenge
when he says, "You Christians, you do not know your own gospel.
You have made it into another religion. You have made another
religion out of Christianity." This statement shocked me.
Says he: " To most of the people in India, the church is a
sacred performance. The minister is the great actor. The
audience is the spectator. They do not know really what it is
all about. It is much like it used to be in the Roman Catholic
church where everybody looked at the priest as he was performing.

They did not know why or what for because it was all in Latin.
In awe they watched the great and beautiful performance, while
they sat either as spectators or as endurers who had to endure
certain things in the name of religion."

If the gospel is not made relevant to the people, Christianity becomes a performance. It becomes another religion
that somebody performs in the name of some kind of God over
there, and I quietly, silently endure it.

What then do we mean by the relevance of the gospel? The
relevance of the gospel is dependent on several factors - configuration, conceptualization, contextualization communication
takes place within this triangle.

If the gospel is to be relevant, it must take on its own
configuration. Do not be frightened by that word. It simply
means that it must have an emphasis that touches somehow my needs
or appeals to my aspirations and dreams, or pricks my conscience.
It has been interesting to me to study the book of Acts and to
find that in the book of Acts, while the cross is definitely
present, the emphasis is upon the resurrection. The apostles
were witnesses of His resurrection. Why is that? Why wasn't
that when Paul came first to Corinth? Here he put the cross
into the center. In the book of Acts it is the resurrection
that is in the emphasis. Anyone who has studied the dynamic
movements in Latin America knows that here every dynamic and
expanding movement has either the doctrine of the Holy Spirit
or the Lordship of Christ in the center, or the two, but not the
Saviorhood of Christ.

You say, "That's wrong." No, it is not necessarily wrong
to begin with. If it stays there then it is wrong. The average
Latin American has all his life seen the Savior hanging helplessly on the cross bleeding to death. He has not done him any good.
He seemingly could not help Himself, how can He help me? But
if we come to the Latin with a living, triumphant, risen Lord,
he begins to listen. It is from the Lordship we go into the
Saviorhood of Jesus Christ.

Logically and theologically we should proceed from the
Saviorhood to the Lordship. I agree. On the other hand, we may
have to reverse the procedure in order to touch certain individuals. We may need to begin with the Holy Spirit and from here
lead to the Father and to the Son. This is what we mean by
configuration. In no way is this distorting the gospel of Jesus
Christ. We do not limit the gospel or truncate it. The gospel
is God-given. It is settled in heaven and on earth. However,
is takes on different configurations. Thus Matthew puts the

<u>King</u> into the center, Mark the <u>Prophet</u>, Luke the <u>Priest</u>, John the <u>Son of God</u>.

Some time ago I was privileged to share an hour of fellowship with our dear brother Bakht Singh. As we talked about evangelism and a message for India, I asked him: "When you preach in India, what do you emphasize?" "Do you preach to them the <u>love</u> of God?"

"No," he said, "Not particularly. The Indian mind is so polluted that if you talk to them about love they think mainly of sex life. You do not talk to them much about the love of God."

"Well," I said, "do you talk to them about the <u>wrath</u> of God and the judgement of God?"

"No, this is not my emphasis," he remarked, "they are used to that. All the gods are mad anyway. It makes no difference to them if there is one more who is angry!"

"What do you talk to them about? Do you preach Christ and Him crucified?" I guessed.

"No," he replied. "They would think of Him as a poor martyr who helplessly died."

"What then is your emphasis, do you talk to them about eternal life?"

"Not so," he said, "if you talk about eternal life, the Indian thinks of transmigration. He wants to get away from it. Don't emphasize eternal life."

"What then is your message?"

"I have never yet failed to get a hearing if I talk to them about forgiveness of sins and peace and rest in your heart. That's the product that sells well. Soon they ask me how they can get it. Having won their hearing I lead them on to the Savior who alone can meet their deepest needs."

That is what we mean by <u>configuration of a message</u>. Not in any way does it imply a cutting down of the gospel. It seeks to win a hearing in order to present the gospel.

Note, however an inherent danger. Configuration is wise and wins a hearing. However, if you stay with the configuration as I have just outlined it and do not develop it into a full-

orbed gospel message and present the total counsel of God, you
will soon become a sectarian. A lopsided gospel breeds sectarianism. That is how sectarianism begins. That is how
sectarianism develops. It starts usually with a truth, but it
keeps on harping on that one truth until it becomes central
and the exclusive and all-inclusive message.

A second emphasis is conceptualization. By conceptualization we mean to put it into the vocabulary and into the
thought forms of the people. Here we need to be very sensitive.
I do believe in the verbal plenary inspiration of the Bible.
That simply means that the words of the Bible as well as the
thoughts and concepts are divinely given. The very words of
the Bible are chosen by the Holy Spirit. Each word is selected
by the Holy Spirit. This is verbal, plenary inspiration. I
firmly hold to it. On the other hand, if we make this a very
rigid and one-sided concept, we cannot even translate the Bible
because it was written in the Hebrew language. This is where
our problem comes in. Finally we have to communicate to the
people in their language. However, when we communicate it to
them in their language, a problem arises. We must remain aware
of this.

This reminds me of an experience in India. I was preaching
on the text "Create in me a Clean Heart, oh God." When I came
to the word, "heart", he translated it by atman. Well, I know
enough of Hinduism that I know what atman means. It means a
part, a personalized part of Brahma. I said to myself, "I got
to get away from that concept and word."

So I chose my next word, the Spirit, "Create in me a Clean
Spirit." The translator, however used the word atman. I chose
the word "soul". He still used the word atman. I tried the
word, "mind" -- he still used the word atman. I finally gave
up. I quoted the text only once or twice more. I did not know
just what to do. I was disturbed over it. When I came to the
end, I asked some of the missionaries what was going on here.

"Well," they said, "we believe that all Christians understood you perfectly all right."

I said, "What if a Brahmin had been here, what would he
have thought?" Whereupon one of the missionaries remarked,
"Well, he would have said, "After all Christianity fits beautifully into Hinduism." Such is the dilemma we meet again and
again.

What can be done? That seemingly is the only word they
have to express the concept. Therefore a conversion of the

concept must take place. You have to put it into their vocabulary. But if you do not convert the concept thoroughly syncretism easily develops. In fact this is how syncretism begins.
This is also how spiritism moves in and occultism thrives. My
brethren and sisters, here are two enemies of evangelicalism.
We have to be on the guard. The one is syncretism, the mixing
of religions and religious intent, the other is spiritism, the
confusion of spirits. It comes on both levels.

I come next to contextualization. This is a new concept.
It is today the most explosive concept. Contextualization has
far-reaching implications and ramifications. Used properly and
accurately it becomes a friend of the gospel and the church.
However, it can be easily misused. Contextualization properly
applied means to discover the legitimate implications of the
gospel text in a given situation. It goes deeper than application. Application I can make or need not make without doing
injustice to the text. Implication is demanded by a proper
exegesis of a text. Most certainly the Bible is meant to
speak to concrete situations. It is existential as well as
historical. To omit the implications is to truncate the
message, to fall short of its actual meaning. Therefore our
question must be not only what did the text mean to the readers
and/or hearers of the time when the message was delivered, but
what does the message mean in our given situation. To make it
only the first is to make it historical, to make it only the
latter is to make it existential. The Bible message must be
both historical and existential. It may be, in addition, pro-
phetic.

Contextualization, therefore is an important hermeneutical
principle and must be carefully heeded. Properly exercised and
applied, it need not be feared. It is perfectly in place to
ask: What did Luke 4:18 mean to the people in the synagogue of
Nazareth when Jesus read it to them and what are its implications for Latin America, Africa, India etc. today? We have to
ask ourselves seriously: Have we truncated the gospel of Jesus
Christ by being narrow and/or simplistic? What is the gospel?
What are its implications and ramifications in today's world?
Does the gospel introduce an explosive dynamic or a progressive,
transforming dynamic that without violence brings about the
will and purpose of God, first in the life of individuals and
gradually works itself into society and social structures?
Such are the legitimate questions we must raise and answer.

The concept "contextualization" however has fallen into
evil hands and upon evil soil. As a result we speak of Western
theology, Asiatic theology, African theology, Latin American
theology. Philosophically and culturally such language is

understandable. Biblically and Christian it is unacceptable,
there is only one kind of theology for the Christian. It is
biblical theology. The Bible is the all determining factor and
final authority in all matters of faith, practice, purpose,
goal and methods of procedure.

The error prevalent today lies in the reversal of an important hermeneutical principle. Too many are reading the Bible
in the light of the circumstances. They are putting the cart
before the horses. Not the word is casting light upon the path
and circumstances, but the circumstances are true meaning and
the message of the word of God.

Of course this is nothing new. For centuries tradition
obscured the word. Then nationalism dimmed its light. Next
higher criticism diminished the message for multitudes. Today
it is non-Christian culturism and immediate circumstances (a
type of existentialism) that seek to erode divine revelation and
relativise the gospel. In this manner contextualization actually
becomes an enemy of the gospel of Jesus Christ.

As an example consider Walter Rauschenbusch, the father of
the so called social gospel. I have read his life story. He
came from a godly home. He started out well in the gospel of
Jesus Christ. However, he soon became so wrapped up in the
social welfare of the people that he contextualized the whole
gospel message in terms of one basic concept, the social needs
of the people. Here was his serious mistake. The same blunders
underlie the Theology of Revolution and the Theology of Liberation.

Note, my brethren, here are the issues that we need to
wrestle with deeply. Configuration, if not balanced by the
total counsel of God, will lead us into a narrow sectarianism.
Conceptualization, if not carefully mastered, will lead us into
syncretism and spiritism. Contextualization, if not girded and
limited carefully, will lead us into a social gospel just as it
has led others into a purely "this world" gospel. These are
some of the issues we as evangelicals need to wrestle with on
a deep and theological level.

I leave two challenges for you. Number one: It is my
deep conviction that in the later seventies and in the eighties,
the major battles will be in the realm of theology of missions,
not in technology and methodology but in the field of theology.
We better train and prepare some specialists along that line
to be able to cope with these issues in the fields on the deepest level. Otherwise, we will become a shallow movement.

Secondly, I leave this challenge: I do believe it is time for IFMA and EFMA to think seriously of <u>a theological commission</u> that wrestles on deep theological levels with these issues, alerting the missions again and again about the things that are going on in the different areas of the world.

I want you to know I have perfect confidence in my national brethren. We will never analyze things on a deeper level than such men as Dr. Philip Teng of Hong Kong does. We have men and minds we can trust and depend on. The brethren are analyzing movements and circumstances on as deep a level as we ever will. The Seoul Declaration is a good example of this. I have full confidence in them. However, they are so few. We need to give them all the support and all the help we possibly can.

So here are issues on the organizational operational levels and on the theological levels. Do not permit these to become frustrations or abstracts to hinder the work of God. God help you to wrestle with them as men of God.

14
EVANGELISM IN THE FUTURE
by Luis Palau

I praise God for missionaries. It's so good to be here and talk with so many missionaries and ex-missionaries. I'm one of those people who get very upset with anyone who criticizes missionaries.

My dad is in heaven thanks to a missionary who came all the way from Europe to Buenos Aires, Argentina where we were living. I remember that missionary so well. He was a Britisher, he didn't speak Spanish very well, he insisted on dressing as if he were back in cold Scotland, down there in warm Argentina.

As a young boy, sitting there listening to him preach, I often wondered, "Why doesn't he take off some of those vests and extra socks and be comfortable?"

However, different as he was, he was responsible for my dad coming to know the Lord. My grandmother and many other people from that part of Argentina are in heaven, thanks to him.

I love missionaries because I was led to the Lord by a missionary. The fellow who led me to Christ never did learn to speak Spanish decently. He wasn't the warm, friendly type as most Argentineans are -- he was reserved and formal. But I really don't mind because thanks to him, I belong to Christ.

It is because of missionaries that I am in crusade evangelism. The missionary that got me out of my little church and inspired me toward crusade evangelism was not a completely "successful" missionary. Yet, he gave me a love for the whole

---

Luis Palau, presently the President of Overseas Crusades, is a native of Argentina, a graduate of Multnomah School of the Bible, and is widely known for his outstanding crusade ministry in Latin America, the United States and Europe.

Body of Christ and I'm in the ministry of winning souls, thanks
to him.   I thank God for that missionary, I love him, and I love
his supporters.

Now, I'd like to publicly thank all of you (EFMA-IFMA participants) for your prayers, particularly for Continente '75.   The
Lord was gracious and blessed in a big way during Continente '75,
the crusade from Managua, Nicaragua last year.   According to the
Costa Rican organization, Difusiones InterAmericanas (Inter-Ameri-
can Broadcasting) that is connected with LAM, they estimate that
80 million people heard the Gospel broadcast from Managua.

What a thrill this is.   Many of your missions supported us
financially.   Many of the missionaries that you represent participated in the follow-up and in publicity, and the radio and
television broadcasts.   I really praise God for that help.   Some-
day I hope that many of you will be able to come to one of our
crusades.

Tonight, I stand here before you, having been saved through
missionaries, motivated toward crusade evangelism by missionaries,
and supported in my crusade ministry by a missionary organization,
now as president of that missionary organization.   It's somewhat
awesome to me, even yet, but I am excited about it.   I believe
this is a wonderful opportunity to trust the Lord to keep me
active in evangelism and use me to encourage the missionaries in
our mission.

WORKING TOGETHER

In Latin America, more and more, when we hold press conferences, leftists, and pro-Marxists newsmen often attack either
our relationship with Americans or the fact that the missions
aren't all together.

With much authority, I say, "We do work together.   We do
get together.   We have our differences, we have our disagree-
ments on unimportant matters, but at heart, we are one."

That is a real blessing.   If the unity that we enjoy in
fellowship here can also be experienced on the field, by our
missionaries together, it gives one a fantastic authority when
you come to a city for evangelism.   It's powerful and very
helpful.

VISION

I'd like us to look at a famous passage we use many times
in mission conferences.   This passage spoke to me about evangelism in the future.   Matthew 9:35-10:1a.

And Jesus went about all the cities and villages,
teaching in their synagogues and preaching the gospel
of the kingdom, and healing every disease and every
infirmity.

When he saw the crowds, he had compassion for them,
because they were harassed and helpless, like sheep
without a shepherd.

Then he said to his disciples,   'The harvest is plentiful, but the laborers are few;

pray therefore the Lord of the harvest to send out
laborers into his harvest.'

And he called to him his twelve disciples and gave
them authority.

The first word that comes out of this text concerning evangelism in the future is the word "vision". If we are going to
think of evangelism in the next ten to twenty years, as the
Lord gives us life and energy, we need to catch a big vision of
what could happen through the power of the Holy Spirit.

When I was a boy in Argentina, there was still much persecution. Our little assemblies were all very small. When we set
up a tent for special meetings, a crowd of 100 people seemed
tremendous.

As I became a teenager, I began to have a passion to spread
the Gospel. My friends and I began to pray. My missionary
friend began teaching me to have a big vision -- to pray first
for myself and my family, then our small assembly, then past
that to the world's millions.

It seemed unreal then to pray, "Lord help us to preach to
millions". I didn't even tell my mother about this vision --
she might have said, "My boy is getting a big head".

But how exciting to see, twenty years later, how God is
responding to those prayers. I believe that together, as a
Body, we can look to the Lord for even greater things for the
glory of God.

The scripture tells us that Jesus went "about all the cities
and villages, teaching in their synagogues and preaching the
gospel of the Kingdom". Jesus Christ went everywhere to spread
the Gospel.

My desire is that, in this generation, the Lord will give
us, as a Body, the faith to project big things. Years ago,
when I was a missionary intern in Detroit, Michigan, I heard a
TEAM missionary speak on Pakistan. He spoke on the difficulty
of reaching the Muslim world. As a Latin, just up from the
South, all I could think of was my part of the world.

The missionary from Pakistan began to tell stories of
Muslims who had been converted to Christ. One man had gone
through beatings, and had to go into hiding. As he talked,
God gave me a great passion to pray for the Muslims.

Since then I continue to pray that the Lord will open doors
in that part of the world. I can almost see crowds gathering
in the Muslim world to hear the Gospel of Jesus Christ. Somehow I believe the Lord is going to do it. I feel we should ask
the Lord, "Lord, do it!" God commands us to go and evangelize
and that means it can be done!

We have seen things happen in our generation, particularly
in Latin America, that prove we ought to believe the Lord can
do it -- that we can project, by faith, an impact of the Gospel
on the Muslim world.

When we were young in Argentina, and we prayed for some of
the things that have now taken place, people thought we were
"nuts"! "What a big head these boys have. Do they think they
can get on television and talk to millions of people?" they
wondered. But look what the Lord has done!

Just recently we were in Paraguay, conducting a crusade.
Paraguay is now a relatively easy country, but it hasn't always
been that way. When I told Dr. Billy Graham that we were going
to Paraguay, he said, "Oh boy. Watch out, I was there several
years ago and it was rough."

There was nothing but trouble when he went to Paraguay.
Troublemakers were preparing to form a parade and march to the
stadium to cause havoc. Providentially a storm intervened. And
this was only fifteen years ago.

However, when we were in Paraguay, it was absolutely open.
There wasn't a Paraguayan that didn't know an evangelistic
crusade was taking place. I visited the American Ambassador and
he was well informed of the crusade. From the President, to
the government officials, to the humblest person, all felt the
impact of the Gospel. When we left the country, the President
sent this word: "You conquered", indicating that much of
Paraguay had been influenced.

One might say, "Because of this or that, the door was opened". For whatever reason, it doesn't matter -- the door was open. It was exciting to see the hunger for the Good News and the openness. We could have continued the crusade for weeks. When the crusade began, there were only 3500 evangelical church members. In only 12 days, almost 5,000 people made a committment to Christ. The evangelical community was doubled.

If this happened in Paraguay, why can't it happen in Arabia? Why can't it take place in Communist countries? I believe we must use the gift of faith to say, "Lord open these countries." Then believe He will do it.

At Lausanne, Switzerland during the World Evangelization Conference, many of us heard the story of the Bible Society representative in Lebanon.

He had met the Head of State of a Middle East State at a Christian hospital. Bravely he offered the official a Bible. "Wonderful," the official replied. "I love the Bible."

A little startled, the Bible Society man said, "Why do you love the Bible?"

The official said, "My dad had a Bible. He died, believing in Jesus. He had to keep the Bible hidden, however."

"How did he happen to have a Bible?" asked the missionary.

"Well, my father always went to a Christian hospital when he was ill. One day he noticed a Bible on the table and he began to read it. Soon he believed in the Lord. When he came home, he read the Bible to us all the time. When you come to my country, I would like you to come and read the Bible to me."

Naturally the first chance he had, the Bible Society man went to this official's country and asked for an audience. The official welcomed him, the missionary read the Bible with him and they prayed together. This was all in private.

The next time the missionary went to visit the Head of State, the official told him, "I'm going to let everyone know that I love the Bible." Gathering his ministers together, he said, "This is a good friend of mine from Lebanon who visits me from time to time and he reads the Bible to me. I want him to read the Bible now and all of you are to listen." So, they heard the Scripture.

What God can do! We feel the door is closed, many times.
We feel there is no hope, but God is working. Brothers, I am
asking the Lord to give me a vision, a passion, and a gift of
faith to believe that doors can be opened in places that,
humanly speaking, appear impossible.

NO ONE ASKED

In December of 1975 I was invited to give the opening
address at a marvelous gathering called Mission '76 in Switzerland. There were 3,000 college students from all over Europe.
One day there was a press conference. For some reason, it
seemed to drag, just empty questions, so I turned to the newsmen and said, "You know, as a Latin American I get very upset
about Europe."

"Why?" they asked.

"Well, you speak about 'Free Europe', but this is not
'Free Europe'. I cannot get on TV here and preach about Christ.
I cannot buy radio time for the Gospel. That's not free."

I went on for several minutes on the subject. After the
conference, I went up to one of the leaders of the Swiss Government who happened to be there and said, "Sir, I want to apologize. I may have said too much." (This man was a Protestant.)

"Don't apologize," he told me. "You shook me up."

"Well, was I right or not?" I asked him.

"You're right and not right," he replied. "You're right
that in Switzerland we have seldom had that kind of Gospel
preaching on the air. But you know something? I have authority
to open up TV and radio, but I've been at this for 30 years and
no one has ever come to ask me if they could get on radio or TV
to preach the Gospel. No one, ever!"

Just between us, I believe that many times that is the case.
We take it for granted that nothing is going to happen for God -
and nothing does. We have absolute confidence that nothing is
going to happen -- we even proclaim it!

Certainly there are many closed doors. But many doors are
not as closed as we think they are. I feel we should have a
boldness and a faith to move out and do things that the Lord
could use to open doors.

Latin America seems to be so open, so easy these days. It wasn't easy 20 years ago! But the Lord opened it up and I believe many of the open doors are due to steps of faith taken by men and women of God.

PRIORITIES

The second emphasis we notice in this passage (Matthew 9:35) is "priorities". "And Jesus went about all the cities and villages, teaching in their synagogues and preaching the gospel of the kingdom and healing every disease and every infirmity."

I believe we must have our priorities really clear in the next few years in evangelism. First, Jesus was 'teaching'. That is ministry to the Body of Christ. Building the Body, mobilizing it, awakening its gifts. Secondly, He was 'preaching' -- that is to the lost. Thirdly, He was involved in social action, 'healing every disease and every infirmity'.

There is a tendency in the US to make Americans feel guilty because of the hunger in the world. As if it were some American plot that there is no rain in, say, Africa -- or that all the cattle are dying somewhere. As if the CIA were responsible -- or the missionaries had done it. As though it were the fault of American missions that people are dying of hunger!

We must keep our priorities straight. No matter what anyone says, the ministers and the believers in Latin America want more evangelism -- they want more Bible teaching. This is what we hear from them. These things are all important -- teaching, preaching, and social action, but in that order.

In view of this, evangelism in the future will be tied to Biblical church growth prinicples. Planting churches and starting new congregations is the most exciting thing in the world. I love to preach to crowds in a bullring, or on television, but my greatest joy is to see new local churches springing up where there were none. It's so good to bring in the sheep and gather them in the barns -- see them gathered in there, loving each other and growing in the Lord.

Our Rosario Plan in Rosario, Argentina resulted in 46 new local congregations beginning. I'm going to encourage our mission and other missions to keep on doing evangelism, tied in with church growth programs, thus seeing thousands of new churches started.

I would like to encourage you to start new fields -- send out more missionaries, with a view of planting churches. Also,

I believe there should be more theological education carried on in Latin America. There are never enough ministers to do the job there. If we could just encourage more people to go to seminaries and Bible Schools.

COMPASSION

"When He saw the crowds, He had compassion for them, because they were harassed and helpless, like sheep without a shepherd." (Matthew 9:36)

One thing I am asking the Lord, in my planning and charting is that I will not lose my compassion and warmth for the lost. It's easy to forget. It's easy to get in front of a TV camera to preach and "get plastic". To begin to think of numbers and statistics. To forget the suffering of people. The Lord Jesus had compassion on them.

Why? Because "they fainted". RSV says, "they were harassed". They were weak and pushed around. This is so true in Latin America. I'm sure it's true in Africa, even in Europe, in spite of the facade of strength and sophistication. People really suffer. How helpless they are.

What a joy to cry and pray for them with a tender heart. I feel that evangelism in the future demands we keep compassion for souls on fire. Many of us in executive positions have to deal with so much paper work, personnel, and fund raising. We deal with computers, write prayers letters -- and sometimes may forget those who are suffering, who are harassed, who are like sheep without a shepherd.

In our crusades one important ministry I love is the "Family Counseling Centers". In each crusade city we have at least one of these centers. In Rosario there were five. They are manned by the nationals who have been trained by our team members. At the Asuncion, Paraguay Crusade there were up to 70 people lined up outside, waiting to talk with a counselor. I remember one particular couple I counseled very well. He was an attorney, the brother of an M.D. who was on the Crusade Committee.

They were a young couple, both barely 30. As we sat down together, their very appearance made me so sad. Eyes downcast, neither would look at each other or directly at me. They were terribly embarrassed, yet something had driven them to come for help.

His attitude was typically Latin. He had been unfaithful, commiting immorality as a matter of course from University days on. He never thought of the hurt he had caused his wife.

Then, all of a sudden, his wife began taking classes at the University. A friend of her husband's became coyly friendly -- sympathizing with her, "You poor thing, so beautiful, so young, and your husband is fooling around on the side behind your back...." (You can guess the 'old line'.)

The outcome was predictable. Soon the wife too fell into adultery. Now, here they sat before me, both ashamed, miserable, looking for a solution to their dilemma. What suffering I saw in their faces!

We talked together and read God's Word. Then I made them confess everything to each other, every single thing. Tears began to flow as the three of us knelt together. Impulsively they embraced and they asked God to forgive them. They turned to each other and asked forgiveness from each other. Was I broken up right there!

For evangelism in the future we must keep a heart of com-passion. Keep a warm heart, so that the power of the Holy Spirit will be upon us and we will cry for souls. Be ready to weep and cry for the suffering of people without Jesus Christ.

One day I remember we were guests at the Baton Rouge, LA Billy Graham Crusade. We were having coffee with Dr. Walter Smyth who is Director of Crusades. He's been with Mr. Graham's Team for over 25 years and has seen hundreds of thousands "come forward" to receive Christ.

That morning we were reviewing the previous night's crusade meeting. A downpour had sent home 25,000 of the 50,000 in the stadium. Still many had come forward at the invitation. Tears in his eyes, Dr. Smyth recalled how that night, long after the meeting, the policeman in charge of Mr. Graham's personal se-curity had come knocking on Mr. Graham's motel door. "I want to be saved," he said.

Mr. Graham invited him in, explained the Gospel and, on his knees, the man received Jesus Christ into his life. He rushed home to his wife, woke her up, saying, "Woman, woman, I've been saved!" She began to cry. For years she had prayed for her husband's conversion.

As he told the story, tears streamed down Dr. Smyth's cheeks. He cried like a baby right there in the coffee shop, telling the story. It moved me profoundly. Right then, in my heart I prayed, "Oh, God, keep me that way. Even if I see a million come forward to receive you, I want to have a tender heart and be able to cry over them."

URGENCY

"Then he said to his disciples, 'The harvest is plentiful, but the laborers are few; pray therefore the Lord of the harvest to send out laborers into his harvest.'" (Matthew 9:37-38)

He says, "The harvest is plentiful". It's ready now! Therefore, we must go get it now. Many times the tendency is to point out the mistakes that are made, forgetting that the harvest is sitting out there -- ready. While we sit around discussing problems, mistakes, and concepts, some humble guy who can't even read or write is winning souls!

In Paraguay, at the Asuncion Crusade, I met one of the counselors -- an older man, humanly unimpressive. The brother who introduced us said, "This man has personally led more people to Christ than anyone I know, and he can't read or write. His nephew, a boy, goes with him to fill out the decision cards. He is an excited soul-winner. He even stops people on the streets to tell them about Jesus Christ."

Illiterate though he was, one of our team members trained him for special family counseling. What happened? He led three M.D.'s to Jesus Christ! This man had a vision of what is important -- all he knows is that the Lord said, "Go evangelize" and that's exactly what he's doing.

I believe we need to prepare for the future when the doors may not be open any longer. The past ten years have been nearly free from confrontation, but there are indications that opposition is coming. You sense it in some countries more than others.

SEND SERVANTS

In verse 37, the Lord Jesus says to pray that the Lord of the harvest will send out laborers. He doesn't say, "Pray that the Lord will send out executives." It's laborers.

This is what we must encourage our missionaries to be. Not necessarily the leader of the national church, but encourage them to be servants -- working with the nationals, winning people to Jesus Christ. To cooperate on an international team basis.

This is the most powerful combination of team forces. It has happened on our team. When I'm asked in a press conference,

"Do you use American money for your crusades?", I say, "Yes, I
use American money and Mexican money and Argentina money. I get
money for crusades from all these countries."

They ask, "Do you have Americans on your team?"

I reply, "Yes, I do. I have Americans, Guatemalans, Ecua-
dorians, Argentineans, Dominicans. We want to have team members
from every country." This really calms things down at the press
conference!

We tell them, "We believe the Body of Christ is international.
There are no barriers to the Gospel. We are here to prove that
there can be one body."

One of the greatest contributions that an American missionary can make for evangelism in the future is to work with the
nationals in three basic ways:

1. Build a platform for nationals. This is what Overseas
Crusades did for me. It was a great blessing and help to me. I
had dreamed of being an evangelist, but I needed a platform, a
base from which to operate. American missionaries can quietly
build a platform behind the national and be a great blessing as
part of an international team.

2. Life building. I imagine Africa and other countries
are the same, but I will speak for Latin America. Our spiritual life is very weak in Latin America. There are many souls
being saved, but the spiritual life is weak. There is much
falling into immorality, too much weakness over money among our
Latin people.

A missionary, being a part of an international team,
could stay in the background, praying and counseling these
nationals. This is what my missionary friends did for me --
they spent hours and hours training me, helping me be holy,
praying with me and teaching the Word. Missionaries can be
a part of an international team and help in that way. They
will be part of the harvest, but in a position as a team member, with the nationals.

3. Intellectually. Many of the people from the Third
World are not highly intellectually developed. Many, many pastors have only a high school primary education. Very few have
college. The missionary can help by providing books, encouraging the nationals to read magazines and helping further the
intellectual development in many ways.

I believe international teams would be the best way for evangelism to operate during the next ten to twenty years. Then even the Communists could not fight you. There would be Americans, nationals, everyone working together. Prove our oneness by our actions. What power and authority this will demonstrate.

If we could translate our togetherness here at this conference into humble cooperation on the mission field, brothers, the impact would be fantastic! We could face the critics and say, "We are united. We are one. We believe and trust the same Lord Jesus."

During the crusade in Paraguay, I was so impressed by some of the missionaries who were helping. They were not sitting up on the platform -- no, they were out passing out decision packets, helping with the ushering, welcoming people. I thought, "Lord, what a blessing to have these missionaries doing that. What an example!"

The Crusade Committee too, made up of many professionals -- doctors, lawyers, and engineers. But they were doing the same. I am convinced that it was the example of the missionaries, doing the simple servant jobs, that made the others have this servant attitude.

AUTHORITY OF HOLINESS

"And he called to him his twelve disciples and gave them authority." (Matthew 10:1)

In Latin America, particularly, I believe the Body of Christ needs to be taught holiness. There is much fooling around. We need missionaries, who are holy themselves, who will come down there and live holy lives and teach others how to live holy lives.

The passage says, "he called to him his twelve disciples." Now, it isn't possible to get close to the Lord if you aren't holy. Then He gave them authority. There is authority in holiness. A holy person may not be brilliant, not be extremely eloquent, but there is a power evident in a holy person.

Robert Murray McCheyne once wrote, "A holy man is an awesome weapon in the hands of God." Think about that! Missionaries should go as humble servants to help people live holy lives, both by their examples and by teaching and praying with them.

This message has just been sharing from my heart some of the blessings of God that we've seen in evangelism and in Latin America. I believe God wants to work in the Middle East, in Europe, in the Muslim world, in Egypt, all over the world.

Last June I was privileged to preach in the United Kingdom for a whole month. We received invitations for crusades in Scotland and in Wales. This year we will be going to Germany and to Wales.

All this is so amazing! I'm praying that God might use me and that what He's doing in Latin America He will do in Europe too. It was a Britisher that brought us the Gospel in Argentina. Now we're going back there. It's a thrilling thought.

This demonstrates that the time has come when international teams and international missions are becoming a reality. Where we will go from all nations to all nations. It's very exciting.

I see the next ten years, God willing, as probably the most exciting and productive years yet, if we put into practice all the things we teach and believe -- church growth, evangelism, theological education by extension, international teams, in the power of the Holy Spirit, the power of holiness, and the power of a servant heart. If we pray unceasingly for the lost this can be the greatest harvest time of our lives.

APPENDIX

INTRODUCTION

At one of the sessions Mr. Donald Hamilton, Executive Director of The Association of Church Missions Committees spoke of the role of the local church in missions and the ministry of his association to those churches.

One of the functions of ACMC has been to create discussion among churches through the use of a questionnaire called "Forum". The participating churches answer questions which are then tabulated and distributed by ACMC. The May issue of Forum dealt with evaluating the effectiveness of the missionary and missions organizations. (A compendium of the replies can be secured by sending $1.00 to ACMC, 1021 East Walnut, Suite 202, Pasadena, CA 91106)

In response to the May Forum, Dr. Wesley Duewel, President of OMS International wrote ACMC to explain some of the complexities of evaluating missionary personnel. Mr. Hamilton responded by giving some of the concerns of the local churches about this matter. The conference requested that the exchange be included in this book. The writers have agreed to this arrangement and their letters (slightly revised) are presented here.

OMS INTERNATIONAL, INC.
P.O. Box A
Greenwood, Indiana 46142

June 16, 1976

Association of Church Missions Committees
1021 East Walnut, Suite 202
Pasadena, CA 91106

Dear Friends:

Your May 1976 bulletin, Volume 2, Number 4, reached us on
June 11. I would like to respond to your questionnaire, which
is primarily addressed to local church committees.

1. It is thrilling to have local churches become more and
more involved in world evangelization. All worthy missionary
organizations encourage this.

2. It is important that local churches realize their own
limitations in supervising work on the field or at times even
properly evaluating the total program. This is why God has
raised up missionary societies. Anyone who is working on a
strictly independent basis and who is unable to work in the
fellowship of other missionaries in a proper organization is
naturally to be questioned and his work very carefully evaluated.
Those working within the fellowship of responsible missionary
organizations should be evaluated not only in the light of what
they are doing but also in the light of what the organization is
doing. On any given field that organization's missionaries
need to work together as a team, and if each one does his
assigned part with the proper spirit then he shares in the total
result. Thus, if all lift the load in prayer, the one who coordinates the follow-up shares just as much in the new decisions
for Christ as the one who coordinates the campaign or the one
who gives the actual invitation. Similarly, those at the home
base of the society who live on the same sacrificial allowance
as the folks on the field, many of whom would prefer being on
the field but are at the headquarters because they were appointed to this work, share no less in the field results if they
maintain the same spirit of prayer, sacrifice, and faith.

Thus, in our own society, the president of the society and
the newest recruit in the homeland all get the same allowance.
There is no variation for seniority, administrative position,
or anything of the kind. It is all on the basis of a sacrificial missionary allowance, and it is also thoroughly equated

with what the people get on the field, coordinated through the services of Organization Resources Counselors, so that those on the field get an exact equivalent amount. Thus throughout the entire society, all share equally. A secretary in the office at home could be made to feel that she is not sharing in the real action on the field if the questionnaires are improperly worded. But if she is equally effective in her part of the team effort, she is just as much a missionary and is sharing equally in the results with the ones who seemingly are out on the front lines. In sacrificial team work, the front line is right where everyone works who is totally involved. It is not where the more glamorous point seems to be or where the more visible action seems to be.

3. Questionnaires concerning the team effort should not be addressed to individual missionaries but to the organization, for the following reasons:

a. The individual missionary may not have at his finger-tips all the information which is available at the field or society headquarters.

b. The individual missionary many times does not have secretarial service available to him. And to give a total picture requires often a very long explanation. It is often unfair to judge a field on the basis of a yes or no question or on the basis of a one-line answer. You have to understand where the program was, where it has progress-ed to, and where it is reaching in its objectives. No evaluation is satisfactory unless it is in the total con-text. It is unfair to expect missionaries to give all this information, and especially if it is a new missionary who is just getting rooted on the field and does not have all the background.

c. As more and more individual churches are writing for detailed information, this can take a disproportionate amount of time of the individual missionary. An average missionary in our organization, for example, will have at least 30 supporting churches and may have as many as 50 or more. The amount of the support in each of these may vary a great deal, but it is thrilling to have the prayer of such a large group behind them. But if the missionary is going to answer detailed questionnaires from all of these, he will be kept from a number of his assignments on the field. You may get the reaction we had from one of our missionaries who said, in effect: "Do you want me to get on with the job of winning souls, or do you want me to answer these pages of information you want?" We fully

believe in adequate reporting, but once the missionary has
prepared his report, if he is working through a proper organization that report could then be conveyed to those who
want information about it through the society's headquarters, and the missionary himself should not be expected
to take the time to write these often very involved letters
which must accompany every questionnaire. This is why
societies have headquarters, to handle these time-consuming
details on behalf of the missionary who is expected to get
the job done.

May I express one further concern. Inasmuch as the members
of a mission committee may change repeatedly, depending upon
the stability of the type of organization of the local church
and the amount of rotation which they plan into their program,
it is often doubtful whether the local committee has adequate
experience to properly evaluate the effectiveness or non-effec-
tiveness of a particular type of service. May I give a personal
example:

On the field where I was directing our own work, I prepared extensive questionnaires and the field committee spent
three days prayerfully seeking God's face and evaluating the
society program in the light of this questionnaire. We were
asking God why results were more slow in a part of India which
was comparatively unresponsive to the gospel. We asked whether
we should only work where God is powerfully working and leave
hundreds of villages without one Christian witness of any denomination whatever; or whether we should keep a part of our
personnel in a continuing witness operation, even in the less
responsive areas. There was much heart searching and a great
attitude of humility and seeking God's guidance. A very careful resolution was drafted at the close of the three days, in
which we stated that while we knew we could always be more
spiritual, more prayerful, and more anointed of God, yet as we
had searched ourselves we could find nothing in our unity as
a team, in our commitment to God, in the methods we used, or
any other point where we could evaluate that would be an adequate reason for the comparative unresponsiveness of this
section of India.

We had just gone to our homes when I received a long tape
from a "missions leader" of considerable influence. In the
accompanying letter he asked me to play this tape for all of
our missionaries and asked them to search their hearts before
God. When I played the tape, I found he was saying something
is wrong with you missionaries--either you are not walking with
God or you are not preaching scriptural truth; you are not
prayerful; you are disunited; or in some way you are out of God's

will or you would be having the same kind of success that
people are having in other places. He then quoted examples. As
a field leader, I could not conscientiously break the heart of
my missionaries by playing that tape before them. I knew the
dear home leader, who happened to be from the British Isles,
just did not know enough about missions even though he thought
he was very well informed. In that same area today we are
seeing results out of all proportion with anything we saw for
the first 25 years. We were laying the foundation then. Today
we are reaping the harvest. I do not believe it is because we
have changed our message or methods or anything else. But I
believe we are doing a better job of focusing prayer from the
homeland on the field than ever before. We were then praying,
weeping, and fasting on the field, pleading for souls, and I
trust they are still doing it today.

When I came home from the field, I recruited 1,000 people
to spend 15 minutes a day in prayer. When I was in India this
January, someone asked me, "Are you surprised at what God is
doing?" I replied, "I certainly am." I was rebuked by the
answer I received: "You ought not to be." "Why?" I asked.
And the reply was, "Don't you remember the hundreds and hundreds
of people you recruited to pray? Why are you surprised when
God is answering prayer?"

Now I submit to you that many a missions committee could
conclude that a certain missionary in a certain place, or perhaps a whole team, was ineffective, out of God's will, not
worthy of support, etc., if they did not have a very extensive
background of mature understanding. Judson went for seven years
before he had one convert in Burma.

It is because of reasons such as these that I feel one of
the important things for missions church committees to remember
is that there are coordinating organizations. We have two such
evangelical organizations in this country: the Evangelical
Foreign Missions Association, which is a commission of the
National Association of Evangelicals and which coordinates perhaps nearly a hundred missionary organizations. The other is
the Interdenominational Foreign Mission Association. Many
mission organizations are inadequately administered and would
not be accepted by these organizations for membership. This in
itself is a form of accreditation which is highly important,
and acceptance of a group by EFMA or IFMA is always done very
prayerfully and carefully.

If there is dissatisfaction with the work of a given organization, then the EFMA or IFMA should be approached and the
matter should be examined. But I doubt if the local church has

sufficient background to serve as its own accrediting organization. It is no more logical for them to do this than for them
to serve as an accrediting organization for a theological
school or a Christian college. Those who give their lives to
this thing are best qualified to serve on the accreditation
committee for such purposes, and in such accreditation it is
always done by an impartial committee that does not involve the
people of its own organization. If you feel that EFMA or IFMA
is inadequate in their procedures, then I feel that is where
changes should begin.

As a further illustration, let me point out that every
field in our own society, OMS International, prepares its own
annual plan. In that annual plan there are long-range goals,
immediate goals, and the action plan for the implementation.
Each department on each field has to state these goals and these
objectives, its own action plan, list the accomplishments of the
previous year, list the financial requests, the personnel requests, and all these things. These field plans are not prepared by the field leaders and handed down. They are prepared
by the grass roots. All missionaries involved in the evangelistic phase help prepare the evangelistic plan. All those involved in training, help prepare the educational phase. All
those involved in medical ministries, help prepare the medical
section. All those involved in radio, help prepare the radio
section, etc. Then the field committee sits down together,
surveys, brings in whatever proper balance is needed, and prepares the final draft. This plan is then sent to our headquarters, where it is studied by the leaders of our Field
Ministries Department. Personnel needs for the whole society
are then put together and listed with the appropriate job descriptions. Budgets are approved, altered, or particular por-
tions disallowed. The additional projects needed to carry out
the phase of ministry are approved through the same procedure.
The annual plans for the individual field vary from 20 to 70
pages, single spaced. These are available at the headquarters
to share with anyone who wants to raise questions and to give
interpretations for any questions which might be raised. Major
aspects of these plans are then consolidated and presented to
the board for approval and then the approved plans are con-
firmed back to the field. Then we analyze each field to see
what percentage of the objectives were reached in the previous
year, what are in process of achievement, and which were
dropped, changed, etc. The mission is itself receiving reports
on its missionaries. We are planning to develop a special evaluation instrument for the effectiveness of our missionaries on
the fields. We would be able and willing to discuss any particular missionary in a confidential way with responsible repre-
sentation from any church, but we would have background which

the church committee would not have in its own evaluation. We would have the background of the health record, the psychological screening, and the knowledge of the previous service and effectiveness or ineffectiveness of the individual missionary. I would therefore again say that a missions church committee, rather than try to perform all these functions itself, would probably be better advised to dialogue with the mission headquarters to get the kind of information needed.

This is not to say that we do not want to be cooperative. We certainly do want to cooperate. We want the very deep involvement of local churches. But we must do this in a way that the total cause is most effectively strengthened, with the greatest amount of prayer enlisted to saturate the entire ministry, that unnecessary doubts about an individual are not raised, for this can break the heart of a missionary on the field who is laboring at times in a most difficult place. This evaluation must be done in a way that inadequate judgments are as far as possible avoided. How can we best work together in this? This is my very deep concern.

To encourage each local church to prepare detailed questionnaires may not be the best approach. I am sure you will want to prayerfully consider this whole matter. Wishing you God's blessings.

Yours in Christian fellowship,

Wesley L. Duewel
President

ASSOCIATION OF CHURCH MISSIONS COMMITTEES
1021 East Walnut Street, Suite 202
Pasadena, CA 91106

July 22, 1976

Dr. Wesley L. Duewel
President
OMS International, Inc.
P.O. Box A
Greenwood, IN 46142

Dear Wesley:

I appreciated so very much your letter of June 16 and the
depth of thought that was put into it. So many of the points
that you bring up are very pertinent and do need to be communicated to churches as well as to individuals and others involved
in missions activities.

It is certainly true that the individual church has little
if any realistic way to evaluate individual missionaries or
missions work on the field. It is also true that those who are
involved in service areas of missions activities such as mech-
anics, secretaries, etc., are as much fully involved in missions
activities as any others.

However, it is still a prime responsibility of the missions
committee of the church to help establish purposes and goals of
that church in missions and to be sure that the missions program
of the church is in accordance with these purposes and goals;
likewise, that the balance in the activities as well as the results of their involvement are kept in proper perspective.

Most of what we are trying to do is to help churches identify what are their purposes, goals, structures, and strategies
in missions; to help them establish policies which are workable
within the context of their particular church; to evaluate their
present program against those goals; and to provide a means of
modifying the program to more closely match their purposes and
goals.

As regards a questionnaire for the missions agency and for
the missionaries themselves to fill out, it appears that if a
standardized form could be worked out that would give the agency
all of the information it needed pertaining to the missionary,
the project, and the agency, and the results of this questionnaire openly shared, it could cut down a great deal of the
paperwork and time-consuming, non-standard questionnaires that

are now being devised by more and more churches. Questionnaires may not be the best way of evaluation, but some tool must be devised for this purpose.

ACMC has as its motto "churches helping churches in missions" and thus a great deal of what we are doing, especially through the Forum issue, is providing a platform for churches to talk and share with each other what they have found to work and not work in their missions programs. ACMC is listening carefully to these churches and hearing repeatedly from all over the country their very real concern to evaluate their missions programs in sufficient detail to be sure they are discharging their responsibility well and wisely. There is a great deal of frustration because such an evaluation program is a complex affair. Likewise, there is much naivete in approaching this difficult problem. But it is a real issue and ACMC wants to help any way it can.

I know that in our own church we have evaluated the proportion of our missions program as it pertains to evangelism, nurture and service in our culture or in a cross culture. We are appalled by the high proportion of money going for support and administrative people in this country and how little is actually doing an evangelistic service in reaching unreached peoples who have not heard the gospel. I know that even this is a complex issue with many ramifications, but the church does have the right to determine what its strategy is in missions and to match its dollars with that strategy. This is the reason why at least one ACMC church has indicated that they support both a missionary and a project so that if either the missionary changes in his duties or the project has other people assigned, the whole issue is reevaluated by the church to determine if this is as high a priority for their involvement as other projects and missionaries that have come to their attention. It has classically been the prerogative of the agency to determine where its people go and what they do, and the church is expected to trust the agency in the totality of its deployment of people and choice of project. I feel the ACMC churches are saying that it's time that this changes to more of a partnership or sharing kind of program and that since the missions committees of the churches control the purse strings, they feel they have considerable muscle to enforce their demands.

Likewise, unfortunately, there are bad agencies as well as good agencies. There are some that report the facts as they are, including the diagnostic evaluation and the realistic state of both the missionaries and their projects. There are other agencies whose only communication with the church is pro-

motional. Likewise, there are many churches that are so untrained in missions that they would be unable to receive realistic reports from the field.

There is no question but what a great deal more dialogue
is going to be required about this subject before God's best
answers are found, but the very fact that it is being identified
as a crucial issue that must be faced is healthy.

Let's continue our dialogue on this subject.

Warmly in Christ,

Donald A. Hamilton
Executive Director

ABOUT THE IFMA

Organized in 1917, the Interdenominational Foreign Mission Association is an association of 47 foreign mission boards without denominational affiliation, having a strong conservative evangelical position, and representing some 9,000 missionaries in over 100 countries. It was founded for the purpose of strengthening the effectiveness and outreach of faith missions. As stated in the constitution, its purpose is "to further spiritual fellowship and intercessory prayer; to promote mutual helpfulness and conferences concerning missionary principles and practice; to make possible a united testimony concerning the faith once for all delivered to the saints, and concerning the existing need for a speedy and complete evangelization of the world; and to establish a united voice."

ABOUT THE EFMA

Since its establishment in 1945, the Evangelical Foreign Missions Association has operated as a voluntary association of both denominational and nondenominational foreign mission agencies. EFMA provides its members with opportunities for spiritual fellowship and mutual encouragement through conferences, consultations, conventions and retreats. The EFMA also operates a travel agency which specializes in travel arrangements for missionaries, counsels on tax matters and finances, and is involved with the IFMA in the publication of vital information on modern missions.

IFMA MISSIONS

MEMBER MISSIONS

AFRICA EVANGELICAL FELLOWSHIP
P.O. Box 109, Glen Ridge, N.J. 07028
124 Willowdale Ave., Willowdale, Ont., Can.
M2N 4Y2

AFRICA INLAND MISSION
P.O. Box 178, Pearl River, N.Y. 10965
1641 Victoria Park Ave., Scarborough, Ont., Can.
M1R 1P8

ANDES EVANGELICAL MISSION
P.O. Box 155, Whiting, N.J. 08759
208 Willowdale Ave., Waterloo, Ont., Can. N2J 3M1

ARCTIC MISSIONS, INC.
Box 512, Gresham, Oregon 97030
c/o Native Institute of Canada, Tibbles Road Group
Box, Quesnel R.R. No. 5, B.C., Can. V2J 3H9

BEREAN MISSION, INC.
3536 Russell Blvd., St. Louis, Mo. 63104

BIBLE AND MEDICAL MISSIONARY FELLOWSHIP
241 Fairfield Ave., Upper Darby, Pa. 19082
4028 Sheppard Ave., E., Agincourt, Ont., Can.
M1S 1S6

BIBLE CHRISTIAN UNION
P.O. Box 718, Lebanon, Pa. 17042
554 Main St. East, Hamilton, Ont., Can. L8M 1J3

BIBLE CLUB MOVEMENT
237 Fairfield Ave., Upper Darby, Pa. 19082
Box 4052, Station D., Hamilton, Ont., Can. L8V 4L5

CAM INTERNATIONAL
8625 La Prada Dr., Dallas, Texas 75228
39 Margate, Hamilton, Ont., Can., L8T 1M7

FAR EAST BROADCASTING COMPANY
Box 1, Whittier, Calif. 90608
P.O. Box 2233, Vancouver, B.C., Can. V6B 3W2

FAR EASTERN GOSPEL CRUSADE
P.O. Box 513, Farmington, Mich. 48024
34 Jay St., Toronto, Ont., Can. M6L 2M1

GLOBAL OUTREACH, INC.
Box 654, London, Ont., Can. N6A 4Y4
518 Pearl St., Buffalo, N.Y. 14202

GOSPEL FURTHERING FELLOWSHIP
Lot C-11 Malvern Cts., Malvern, Pa. 19355

GOSPEL MISSIONARY UNION
Smithville, Mo. 64089
132 High Park Ave., Toronto, Ont., Can. M6P 2S4
Box 732, Saskatoon, Sask., Can. S7K 3L7

GREATER EUROPE MISSION
P.O. Box 668, Wheaton, Ill. 60187
P.O. Box 984, Oshawa, Ont., Can. L1H 7N2

HOME OF ONESIPHORUS
3939 N. Hamlin Ave., Chicago, Ill. 60618

INTERNATIONAL CHRISTIAN FELLOWSHIP
1028 College Ave., Wheaton, Ill. 60187
1 Sprucewood Ct., Agincourt, Ont., Can. M1W 1P5

INTERNATIONAL MISSIONS, INC.
Box 323, Wayne, N.J. 07470
P.O. Box 101, St. Catharines, Ont., Can. L2R 6R4

JAPAN EVANGELICAL MISSION
Box 640, Three Hills, Alta., Can. T0M 2A0
9047 Burke Ave., N., Seattle, Wash. 98103

LATIN AMERICA MISSION
285 Orchard Terrace, Bogota, N.J. 07603
3251 Sheppard Ave., E., Scarborough, Ont. M1T 3K1

LIEBENZELL MISSION OF U.S.A., INC.
26 Heath La., Schooley's Mountain, N.J. 07870
236 Finch Ave., E., Willowdale, Ont., Can. M2N 4S2

MISSION AVIATION FELLOWSHIP
P.O. Box 2828, Fullerton, Calif. 92633
P.O. Box 368, Guelph, Ont., Can. N1H 6K6

NORTH AFRICA MISSION
239 Fairfield Ave., Upper Darby, Pa. 19082
205 Yonge St., Toronto, Ont., Can. M5B 1M4

NORTH AMERICA INDIAN MISSION, INC.
1018 No. 5 Road, Richmond, B.C., Can. V7A 4E4
115 Tulalip Rd., N.E., Marysville, Wash. 98270

NORTHERN CANADA EVANGELICAL MISSION
58 - 18th St., E., Prince Albert, Sask., Can. S6V 1C
Box 861, Downtown Sta., Omaha, Neb. 68101

ORINOCO RIVER MISSION
234 E. Colorado Blvd., Pasadena, Calif. 91101

OVERSEAS CHRISTIAN SERVICEMEN'S CENTERS
P.O. Box 10308, Denver, Colo. 80210

OVERSEAS MISSIONARY FELLOWSHIP
404 S. Church St., Robesonia, Pa. 19551
1058 Avenue Rd., Toronto, Ont., Can. M5N 2C6

POCKET TESTAMENT LEAGUE
P.O. Box 368, Lincoln Park, N.J. 07035
3524 Bayview Ave., Willowdale, Ont. M2M 3S5

REGIONS BEYOND MISSIONARY UNION
8102 Elberon Ave., Philadelphia, Pa. 19111
3251 Sheppard Ave. E., Scarborough, Ont., Can.
M1T 3K1

SLAVIC GOSPEL ASSOCIATION
P.O. Box 1122, Wheaton, Ill. 60187
P.O. Box 2, Station K. Toronto, Ont., Can. M4P 2G1

SOUTH AMERICA MISSION
P.O. Box 769, Lake Worth, Fla. 33460

SUDAN INTERIOR MISSION
Cedar Grove, N.J. 07009
10 Huntingdale Blvd., Scarborough, Ont., Can.
M1W 2S5

THE EVANGELICAL ALLIANCE MISSION
P.O. Box 969, Wheaton, Ill. 60187
P.O. Box 980, Regina, Sask., Can. S4P 3B2

TRANS WORLD RADIO
560 Main St., Box 98, Chatham, N.J. 07928
Box 310, London, Ont. N6A 4W1

UNEVANGELIZED FIELDS MISSION
306 Bala Ave., Bala-Cynwyd, Pa. 19004
132 Crescent Rd., Toronto, Ont., Can. M4W 1T9

WEST INDIES MISSION
1607 Ponce de Leon Blvd., Box 343038
Coral Gables, Fla. 33134
Box 333, Brantford, Ont., Can. N3T 5N3

WORLD MISSION TO CHILDREN
P.O. Box 1048, Grants Pass, Ore. 97526
9335 - 94th St., Edmonton, Alberta, Can. T6C 3V6

WORLD RADIO MISSIONARY FELLOWSHIP, INC.
P.O. Box 3000, Opa-Locka, Fla. 33055
3251 Sheppard Ave., E., Scarborough, Ont. M1T 3K

ASSOCIATE MEMBERS

EVANGELICAL LITERATURE OVERSEAS
P.O. Box 725, Wheaton, Ill. 60187

GOSPEL RECORDINGS, INC.
122 Glendale Blvd., Los Angeles, Calif. 90026
2 Audley St., Toronto, Ont., Canada M8Y 2X2

MISSIONARY SERVICES, INC.
P.O. Box 853, Wheaton, Ill. 60187
6935 Airport Hwy. Lane, Pennsauken, N.J. 08109

RAMABAI MUKTI MISSION
P.O. Box 4912, Clinton, N.J. 08809
306-543 Granville St., Vancouver, B.C., Can.
V6C 1X8

SOUTH AMERICAN CRUSADES, INC.
P.O. Box 5664, Fort Lauderdale, Fla. 33310

CANDIDATE MISSIONS

CHRISTIAN NATIONALS' EVANGELISM COMMISSION
1470 N. Fourth St., San Jose, Calif. 95112
P.O. Box 235, Toronto, Ont., Can. M8V 3T2

**INTERNATIONAL CHRISTIAN ORGANIZATION
(INTERCRISTO)**
P.O. Box 9323, Seattle, Wash. 98109

LANGUAGE INSTITUTE FOR EVANGELISM
P.O. Box 200, Alhambra, Calif. 91802

EFMA

American Advent Mission Society
P.O. Box 23152, Mint Hill Station
Charlotte, NC 28212

American Leprosy Missions
297 Park Avenue South, New York, NY 10010

Assemblies of God
Foreign Missions Department
1445 Boonville Ave., Springfield, MO 65802

Baptist General Conference
Board of Foreign Missions
1233 Central St., Evanston, IL 60201

Bethany Fellowship
6820 Auto Club Rd., Minneapolis, MN 55431

Bible Literature International
P.O. Box 477, Columbus, OH 43216

Bible & Medical Missionary Fellowship
4028 Sheppard Ave. E., Agincourt, Ont., Canada

Brethren Church Foreign Missionary Society
P.O. Box 588, Winona Lake, IN 46590

Brethren Church Missionary Board
530 College Ave., Ashland, OH 44805

Brethren in Christ Missions
P.O. Box 149, Elizabethtown, PA 17022

Calvary Evangelistic Mission (WIVV)
P.O. Box A, San Juan, PR 00936

Child Evangelism Fellowship International
P.O. Box 1156, Grand Rapids, MI 49501

Christian Church of North America
Missions Department
P.O. Box 801, Sharon, PA 16146

Christian Literature Crusade
P.O. Box C, Fort Washington, PA 19034

Christian & Missionary Alliance
260 W. 44th St., New York, NY 10036

Christian Nationals' Evangelism Commission
321 Bradley Ave., San Jose, CA 95128

Christian Reformed Board of Foreign Missions
2850 Kalamazoo Ave., S.E.
Grand Rapids, MI 49508

Church of God World Missions
Keith at 25th, N.W., Cleveland, TN 37311

Conservative Baptist Foreign Mission Society
P.O. Box 5, Wheaton, IL 60187

Conservative Baptist Home Mission Society
P.O. Box 828, Wheaton, IL 60187

Eastern European Mission
232 N. Lake Ave., Pasadena, CA 91101

Evangelical Congregational Church
Board of Missions
200 S. Wyomissing Ave., Shillington, PA 19607

Evangelical Free Church
Department of Overseas Missions
1515 E. 66th St., Minneapolis, MN 55423

Evangelical Literature Overseas
P.O. Box 725, Wheaton, IL 60187

Evangelical Mennonite Church
Commission on Overseas Missions
7237 Leo Rd., Fort Wayne, IN 46805

Evangelistic Faith Missions
P.O. Box 617, Bedford, IN 47421

Far East Broadcasting Company
P.O. Box 1, Whittier, CA 90601

Free Methodist Church
General Missionary Board
Winona Lake, IN 46590

Free Will Baptist Board of Foreign Missions
P.O. Box 1088, Nashville, TN 37202

Friends, California Yearly Meeting
Board of Missions
P.O. Box 1607, Whittier, CA 90608

Friends, Eastern Region
Evangelical Friends Church
Foreign Missionary Society
P.O. Box 102, Damascus, OH 44619

Friends, Kansas Yearly Meeting
Board of Missions
P.O. Box 466, Fowler, KS 67844

Friends, Northwest Yearly Meeting
Board of Missions
P.O. Box 190, Newberg, OR 97132

General Baptist Foreign Mission Society
P.O. Box 537, Poplar Bluff, MO 63901

Gospel Films
P.O. Box 455, Muskegon, MI 49443

Grace Mission
2125 Martindale Ave., S.W.
Grand Rapids, MI 49509

Intercristo
P.O. Box 9323, Seattle, WA 98109

International Church of the Foursquare Gospel
Foreign Missions Department
1100 Glendale Blvd., Los Angeles, CA 90026

International Students, Inc.
P.O. Box C, Colorado Springs, CO 80901

Latin America Mission
285 Orchard Terr., Bogota, NJ 07603

Mennonite Brethren Church
Board of Missions & Services
315 S. Lincoln St., Hillsboro, KS 67063

Mexican Mission Ministries
P.O. Box 636, Pharr, TX 78577

Mission Aviation Fellowship
P.O. Box 2828, Fullerton, CA 92633

Missionary Church
Department of Overseas Missions
3901 S. Wayne Ave., Fort Wayne, IN 46807

Nazarene Department of World Missions
6401 The Paseo, Kansas City, MO 64131

North American Baptist General Missionary Society
7308 Madison St., Forest Park, IL 60130

OMS International
P.O. Box A, Greenwood, IN 46142

Open Bible Standard Missions
P.O. Box 1737, Des Moines, IA 50306

Overseas Crusades
265 Lytton Ave., Palo Alto, CA 94301

Pentecostal Assemblies of Canada
Overseas Missions Department
10 Overlea Blvd., Toronto 17, Ont., Canada

Pentecostal Holiness Church
Department of World Missions
P.O. Box 337, Franklin Springs, GA 30639

Pocket Testament League
49 Honeck St., Englewood, NJ 07631

Primitive Methodist International Mission Board
33 N. Market St., Mt. Carmel, PA 17851

Reformed Presbyterian Church of North America
Board of Foreign Missions
Oakdale, IL 62268

South America Mission
P.O. Box 769, Lake Worth, FL 33460

The Navigators
P.O. Box 1659, Colorado Springs, CO 80901

Trans World Radio
560 Main St., Chatham, NJ 07928

United Brethren in Christ
Board of Missions
402 U. B. Building, Huntington, IN 46750

United Fellowship for Christian Service
72 County Rd., Tenafly, NJ 07670

United World Mission
P.O. Box 8000, St. Petersburg, FL 33738

Wesleyan Church
Department of World Missions
P.O. Box 2000, Marion, IN 46952

World Gospel Crusades
P.O. Box 3, Upland, CA 91786

World Gospel Mission
P.O. Box 948, Marion, IN 46952

World Vision International
919 W. Huntington Dr., Monrovia, CA 91016

Worldwide Evangelization Crusade
P.O. Box A, Fort Washington, PA 1903.4

Youth for Christ International
P.O. Box 419, Wheaton, IL 60187